Beginning Node.js, Express & MongoDB Development

Greg Lim

Table of Contents

PREFACE...5

ONLINE COURSE VERSION 7

CHAPTER 1: INTRODUCTION 9

CHAPTER 2: INTRODUCTION TO NPM & EXPRESS 23

CHAPTER 3: BEGINNING OUR BLOG PROJECT 35

CHAPTER 4: TEMPLATING ENGINES 43

CHAPTER 5: INTRODUCTION TO MONGODB.....................................51

CHAPTER 6: APPLYING MONGODB TO OUR PROJECT 61

CHAPTER 7: UPLOADING AN IMAGE WITH EXPRESS 79

CHAPTER 8: INTRODUCTION TO EXPRESS MIDDLEWARE 85

CHAPTER 9: REFACTORING TO MVC 89

CHAPTER 10: USER REGISTRATION 95

CHAPTER 11: USER AUTHENTICATION WITH EXPRESS SESSIONS 107

CHAPTER 12: SHOWING VALIDATION ERRORS 117

CHAPTER 13: RELATING POSTS COLLECTION WITH USERS COLLECTION 127

CHAPTER 14: ADDING A WYSIWYG EDITOR 131

CHAPTER 15: USING MONGODB ATLAS 137

CHAPTER 16: DEPLOYING WEB APPS ON HEROKU 147

ABOUT THE AUTHOR..153

ONLINE COURSE VERSION 155

PREFACE

About this book

In this book, we take you on a fun, hands-on and pragmatic journey to learning Node.js, Express and MongoDB development. You'll start building your first Node.js app within minutes. Every chapter is written in a bite-sized manner and straight to the point as I don't want to waste your time (and most certainly mine) on the content you don't need. In the end, you will have the skills to create a blog app and deploy it to the Internet.

In the course of this book, we will cover:
- Chapter 1: Introduction
- Chapter 2: Introduction to *npm* & Express
- Chapter 3: Beginning our Blog Project
- Chapter 4: Templating Engines
- Chapter 5: Introduction to MongoDB
- Chapter 6: Applying MongoDB to our Project
- Chapter 7: Uploading an Image with Express
- Chapter 8: Introduction to Express Middleware
- Chapter 9: Refactoring to MVC
- Chapter 10: User Registration
- Chapter 11: User Authentication with Express Sessions
- Chapter 12: Showing Validation Errors
- Chapter 13: Relating Post Collection with User Collection
- Chapter 14: Adding a WYSIWYG Editor
- Chapter 15: Using MongoDB Atlas
- Chapter 16: Deploying Web Apps on Heroku

The goal of this book is to teach you Node.js, Express and MongoDB development in a manageable way without overwhelming you. We focus only on the essentials and cover the material in a hands-on practice manner for you to code along.

Working Through This Book

This book is purposely broken down into sixteen short chapters where the development process of each chapter will center on different essential topics. The book takes a practical hands on approach to learning through practice. You learn best when you code along with the examples in the book.

Requirements

No previous knowledge on Node.js development required, but you should have basic programming knowledge.

Getting Book Updates

To receive updated versions of the book, subscribe to our mailing list by sending a mail to support@i-ducate.com. I try to update my books to use the latest version of software, libraries and will update the codes/content in this book. So, do subscribe to my list to receive updated copies!

Code Examples

Where necessary, the relevant source codes links are posted at the end of each chapter.

ONLINE COURSE VERSION

www.greglim.co

This book is all you need to learn Node.js, Express and MongoDB development. But if you are a more visual learner and learn better from absorbing this book's content through an online course, you can get access to the book's online course version **free** by contacting support@i-ducate.com and providing a proof of purchase.

The course content is the same as this book. So, if learning through books is your preferred way of learning, skip this. But if you prefer to learn from videos (and you want to hear my voice), you can visit the following link:

www.greglim.co

CHAPTER 1: INTRODUCTION

Node.js is one of the most popular server-side frameworks. Increasing companies are building their applications with Node.js for example, Wal-Mart, LinkedIn, PayPal, YouTube, Yahoo!, Amazon.com, Netflix, eBay and Reddit. In this book, we will learn about Node.js together with Express and MongoDB and build a blog app from scratch with them. In the process, you will progress from a beginner to where you can build apps effectively using these technologies.

You will learn a range of topics like user authentication, data validation, asynchronous JavaScript, password hashing, Express, MongoDB, templating engines, maintaining user sessions and more.

The App We Will Be Building

We will build a blog app which lets users write blog entries once they sign up with an account (fig. 1.1, 1.2, 1.3).

Figure 1.1 – Home Page

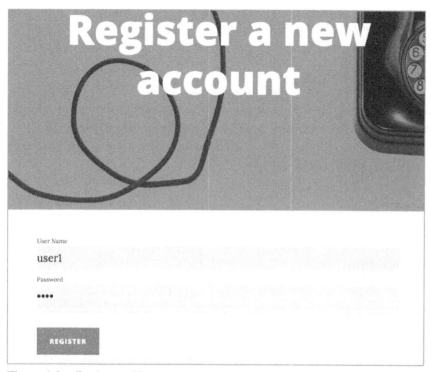

Figure 1.2 – Register a User

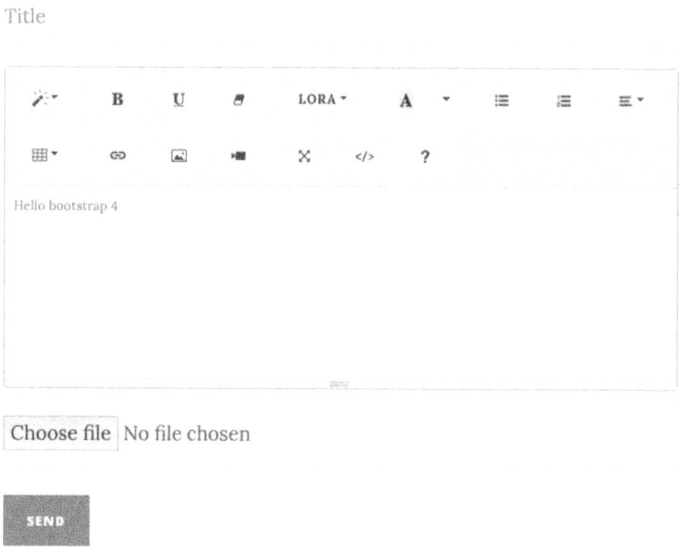

Figure 1.3 – Create Blog Post Form

After the user registers, she can go to the homepage and login with her credentials. The navigation bar will dynamically show different items depending on the user being logged in or out. We will achieve this using the EJS templating engine. Once logged in, the navigation bar will have a 'Log Out' item. There will also be a 'New Post' item where the user can create a new blog post and upload an associated image file. When she goes back to the Home page, her blog entries will be posted there with the username and date posted. Throughout this app, we will learn a lot of concepts and solidify our Node.js, Express and MongoDB knowledge.

What is Node.js?

Before we understand what Node.js is, we need to understand how the Internet works. When a user opens up her browser and makes a request to a site, she is known as a client. The client makes a request of a certain website to a server which upon receiving the request, responds with the content of the requested site to the client who then displays it in her browser. For example, I make a request to amazon.com and Amazon servers responds back with the HTML for amazon.com.

There have been server-side programming languages like PHP, Ruby, Python, ASP, Java and others which helps us respond to browser requests appropriately on the server. Traditionally, JavaScript is used to run only on the browser to provide website interactivity for example dropdown menus. But in 2009, Node.js took V8, Google Chrome's powerful JavaScript engine, out of the browser and enabled it to run on servers. Thus, in addition to the existing server-side languages, developers could now choose JavaScript to develop server-side applications.

What benefits does choosing Node.js as a server-side language bring about?
- Firstly, the V8 JavaScript engine used in Google Chrome is fast and can execute thousands of instructions a second
- Secondly, Node.js encourages an asynchronous coding style making for faster code to manage concurrency while avoiding multithreaded problems.
- Thirdly, because of its popularity, JavaScript offers Node.js access to many useful libraries
- And of course, Node.js provides us the ability to share code between browser and server since they both use JavaScript code. Based on this, developers have created the MEAN stack, an all-JavaScript web application stack consisting of MongoDB (a database controlled by JavaScript) , Express, Angular (a front-end JavaScript framework – I have in fact written a book entirely on Angular) and Node.js. Using JavaScript everywhere is a major benefit of Node.js. In fact, there is also a MERN stack where instead of using Angular, React is used as the front end. In this book, we will cover MongoDB, Express and Node.js, i.e. the MEN stack.

Installing Node.js

To install Node.js, go to *nodejs.org* (fig. 1.4) and download the appropriate version for your Operating System.

Figure 1.4

Installation should be straightforward. Once Node.js has been installed, go to your Terminal and run:

```
node -v
```

This shows the version of Node that you installed e.g. *v14.16.0* (at time of this book's writing). You should also be able to run:

```
npm -v
```

which shows the version of *npm* installed e.g. *6.14.11*. We will revisit *npm* later in this book.

Creating our First Server

We will create our first server to better understand how a request and respond between a client and a server works.

In a code editor of your choice, (I will be using Visual Studio Code in this book), choose a directory location and in it, create a new file called *index.js*. Fill in the below code to create our first server:

```
const http = require('http')
const server = http.createServer((req, res) =>{
    console.log(req.url)
    res.end('Hello Node.js')
})

server.listen(3000)
```

Code Explanation

```
const http = require('http')
```

The *require* function in Node.js helps us to grab the package in Node.js called *http*. *require* is similar to *import* or *include* in other languages. *require* takes the name of a package as a string argument and returns the package.

We require the *http* package and assign it to a variable called *http*. You can then use *http* as you would any object. The general convention is that when you require a module, you put it in a variable that has the same name as the module itself. In our example, we put the *http* module in a variable of the same name *http*. You can of course choose to put it in a variable with a different name, there's nothing enforcing that in code, but it does prevent confusion.

http is one of the built-in packages that Node.js provides to perform actions on the server. Other essential built-in packages that we will cover later is the filesystem access (*fs*) package and the utility function (*util*) package.

```
const server = http.createServer(…)
```

Next, we create and start a server with the *createServer* method from *http* package. *createServer* takes in a

13

function as parameter:

```
const server = http.createServer((req, res) =>{
    console.log(req.url)
    res.end('Hello Node.js')
})
```

The function provided to *createServer* is called a callback function. It will be called when the *createServer* function is completed. When it is called, it will be provided the *request* (*req* – request from browser) and *response* (*res* – response to give back to browser) object in the function. We can do whatever we want with the two objects in the body of the function. In our case, we simply log the request url and after that respond with the text 'Hello Node.js' in the function body.

```
server.listen(3000)
```

Finally, with **server.listen(3000)** we start our server to start taking requests. That is, the server listens on port 3000 for requests. You can specify any port you want, it doesn't have to be 3000. If you are asking what is a port? A port is a specific gateway on the server to host a particular app. For example, if there are multiple apps running on the same server, we specify different port numbers for different apps.

Running index.js

In our case, for any request made to port 3000, we respond with 'Hello Node.js'. To execute the file and start running the server, in Terminal, *cd* to the directory the file is located in and run:

```
node index.js
```

Now go to your browser and enter http://localhost:3000/. *localhost* in this case refers to our computer which is acting as a local server. But suppose the server is hosted on another computer or site, you can imagine that the link would be http://<computer ip>:3000/. In the last chapter of this book, we will learn how to deploy our app on to an external server *Heroku* to make our app available across the Internet.

In your browser, you should see the text 'Hello Node.js' displayed in your browser (fig. 1.5).

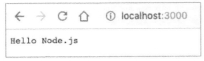

Figure 1.5

This is because we have responded to the request with the code `res.end('Hello Node.js')`. If you look at your Terminal running Node.js, you can see '/' being logged. This is because we have the code `console.log(req.url)` which logs the request url. If you enter http://localhost:3000/noderocks, '/noderocks' will be logged in the Terminal. So, you see that the *req* object contains request data from the browser.

We now have a successful request and respond cycle and I hope that this serves as an example to better understand how a request and respond works between a client and a server.

More on Request and Response

Our app currently responds only with 'Hello Node.js' regardless of the url entered after *localhost:3000*. To have different responses based on different URLs, add the following code in **bold**:

```
const http = require('http')
const server = http.createServer((req, res) =>{
    if(req.url === '/about')
        res.end('The about page')
    else if(req.url === '/contact')
        res.end('The contact page')
    else if(req.url === '/')
        res.end('The home page')
    else {
        res.writeHead(404)
        res.end('page not found')
    }
})
server.listen(3000)
```

To run the newly added code, we have to stop and restart the server with *node index.js*.

Code Explanation

Using an *if-else* statement in the callback function, we check for the request url and depending on its path, we response with different messages. If the url contains '/about', we serve the *about* page. If it contains '/contact', we serve the *contact* page and if it's just '/', we serve the *home* page. If the path does not exist in the *if-else*, we default to the last *else* clause and respond with 'page not found' and also *writeHead*(404).

writeHead writes the status code of the request. Normally, a status code of 200 indicates that the server responded with a successful response. You can see the status code of your request whenever you request a site from the Chrome browser by going to 'Developer Tools under 'View', 'Developer', 'Developer Tools' (fig. 1.6).

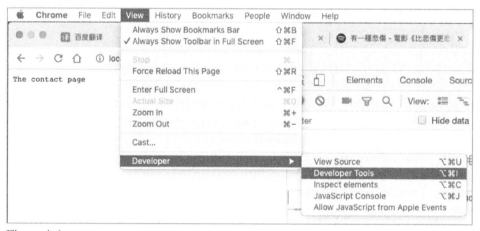

Figure 1.6

To see your request information, in 'Developer Tools', click on 'Network'. Under 'Status', it will show the status code. In figure 1.7, I have requested for '/contact' url, a valid path which returns status code *200* indication 'OK'.

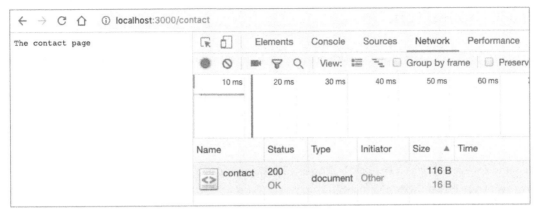

Figure 1.7

If I request for an invalid url like '/contacts' (with an extra 's'), it returns the code 404 indicating 'Not Found' (fig. 1.8).

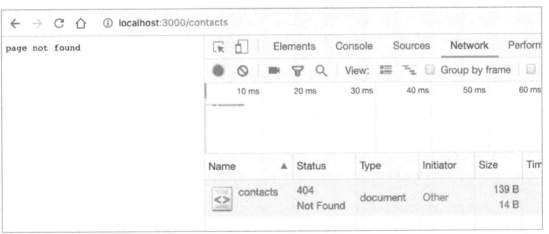

Figure 1.8

With this, we have a way of handling different requests from a client and sending the appropriate response from the server.

Responding with HTML

We have been responding to requests with static text. In a real-world setting, we want to respond with HTML. We illustrate how to do so in this section.

In the same folder as *index.js*, create a new file called *index.html* with the below simple HTML:
```
<h1>Home Page</h1>
```

Do the same for *about.html* (`<h1>About Page</h1>`), *contact.html* (`<h1>Contact Page</h1>`) and *notfound.html* (`<h1>Page Not Found</h1>`).

Back in *index.js*, add the below code in **bold**:

```
const http = require('http')
const fs = require('fs')
const homePage = fs.readFileSync('index.html')
const aboutPage = fs.readFileSync('about.html')
const contactPage = fs.readFileSync('contact.html')
const notFoundPage = fs.readFileSync('notfound.html')

const server = http.createServer((req, res) =>{
    if(req.url === '/about')
        res.end(aboutPage)
    else if(req.url === '/contact')
        res.end(contactPage)
    else if(req.url === '/')
        res.end(homePage)
    else {
        res.writeHead(404)
        res.end(notFoundPage)
    }
})

server.listen(3000)
```

Code Explanation

```
const fs = require('fs')
```

We import a file system module 'fs' which helps us interact with files on our server.

```
const homePage = fs.readFileSync('index.html')
const aboutPage = fs.readFileSync('about.html')
const contactPage = fs.readFileSync('contact.html')
const notFoundPage = fs.readFileSync('notfound.html')
```

The *readFileSync* method from *fs* reads the content of each file and returns it. We store the content in a variable for each page.

```
const server = http.createServer((req, res) =>{
    if(req.url === '/about')
        res.end(aboutPage)
    else if(req.url === '/contact')
        res.end(contactPage)
    else if(req.url === '/')
        res.end(homePage)
    else {
        res.writeHead(404)
        res.end(notFoundPage)
    }
})
```

Instead of *res.end()* containing a static text, *res.end* now contains the HTML page variable.

Running your App

Re-start the server with *node index.js* and we will have HTML presented instead (fig. 1.9). And that is how we respond to requests with HTML using the *filesystem* module.

Figure 1.9

Notice that we have been writing a single JavaScript function for our entire application:

```
...
const server = http.createServer((req, res) =>{
    if(req.url === '/about')
        res.end(aboutPage)
    else if(req.url === '/contact')
        res.end(contactPage)
    else if(req.url === '/')
        res.end(homePage)
    else {
        res.writeHead(404)
        res.end(notFoundPage)
    }
})
...
```

This single function listens to a web browser's requests, either from a computer, mobile phone or any other client consuming our API. We call this function a request handler. When a request comes in, this function looks at the request and decides how to respond. It takes two arguments, an object that represents the request (*req*) and an object that represents the response (*res*).

Every Node.js application is just like this, a single request handler function responding to requests. For small sites, this might seem easy, but things quickly get huge and unmanageable quickly as you can imagine, for example a site like Amazon.com which includes rendering dynamic reusable HTML templates, rendering/uploading of images etc. We explore in the next chapter how Express helps to solve this problem and make it easier for us to write web applications with Node.js.

Summary

In this book, we will build a blog app with Node.js, Express and MongoDB. Node.js allow us to use JavaScript as a server-side programming language which gives us advantages like fast execution and being able to share code between the server and client. We understood how a request and respond cycle between a client and server works by coding and starting up a simple server example. We handled requests and responded appropriately with both text and HTML.

CHAPTER 2: INTRODUCTION TO *NPM* & EXPRESS

Installing Custom Packages with *npm*

In our app from chapter one, we imported packages from Node.js itself e.g., *http*, *fs*. Now the Node.js community have lots of developers who write custom modules/packages that we can use in our own apps. These packages are hosted on a site called *npmjs.com* (fig. 2.1) where you can search to see which is appropriate to use in your own code. We use *npm* (or Node Package Manager) to manage the packages that we download. *npm* is an official helper for Node projects that comes along with Node when we installed it.

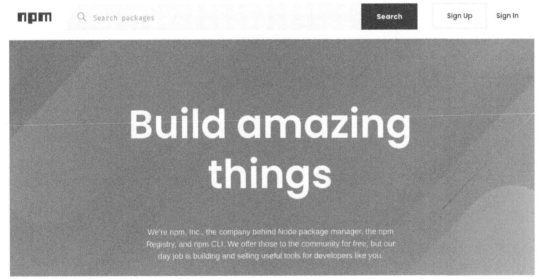

Figure 2.1

One very important custom package we will install is Express. Because vanilla Node.js APIs can be verbose, confusing and limited in features, Express is a framework that acts as a light layer atop the Node.js web server making it easier to develop Node.js web applications. Express is used by many companies. We will see later how it simplifies the APIs of Node.js, adds helpful features, helps organizes our application's functionality with middleware and routing, adds helpful utilities to Node.js's

HTTP objects and facilitates rendering of dynamic HTML views. In the course of this book, we will explore these features in depth.

So, go to *npmjs.com* and search for 'express', there will be instructions on how to install and use the *express* package (fig. 2.2).

Figure 2.2

As mentioned in the site under 'Installation', we have to run *npm install express* to install the *express* package.

Before we run *npm install express*, *npm* requires that we have a file *package.json* to track all packages and their versions used in our app. If you run *npm install express* now without the file, you will get a series of warnings like *"no such file or directory, open ...package.json"*.

To generate *package.json* file, run 'npm init' which will prompt a series of questions about our project (e.g. project name, author, version) to create *package.json* for us. You can of course manually create *package.json* on your own. But *npm init* saves us a bit of time when creating *package.json* files. For now, just press enter for all the questions and at the end, *package.json* (with the contents something like the below) will have been generated for us.

```json
{
  "name": "node",
  "version": "1.0.0",
  "description": "",
  "main": "index.js",
  "scripts": {
    "test": "echo \"Error: no test specified\" && exit 1"
  },
  "author": "",
  "license": "ISC"
}
```

As you can see, *package.json* contains metadata about our Node project like the name of the project, its version and its authors.

Next, proceed to install 'express' with *npm install express*. When installation of *express* is finished, you will notice that a new property *dependencies* has been added to *package.json*.

```json
{
  "name": "node",
  "version": "1.0.0",
  "description": "",
  "main": "index.js",
  "scripts": {
    "test": "echo \"Error: no test specified\" && exit 1"
  },
  "author": "",
  "license": "ISC",
  "dependencies": {
    "express": "^4.16.4"
  }
}
```

Dependencies contain the dependency packages and their version numbers. For now, we have Express version 4.16.4 (at time of book's writing). Each time we install a package, *npm* saves it here to keep track of the packages used in our app.

npm install express installs the *express* package into our app by fetching the latest version of Express and putting it in a folder called *node_modules*. If you look at your app folder, the *node_modules* folder will have been created for you (fig. 2.3). This is where custom dependencies are saved for our project.

Figure 2.3

If you open and explore *node_modules*, you should be able to locate the *express* package. The reason why we see many other packages in *node_modules* even though we only installed *express* is because *express* depends on these other packages and they were installed when *express* was installed. These other packages are dependencies of Express. The file *package-lock.json* tracks the versions of all the dependencies of Express.

Introduction to Express

In this section, we introduce Express and how it makes application development in Node easier and faster. First, we import *express* into our app by adding the below code to *index.js*:

```
const express = require('express')
```

This pulls in the package from the *node_modules* directory.

To appreciate how much easier Express makes development for us, we are going to use Express to repeat what we have previously done in chapter one.

Previously, we created a server and started it with:

```
const http = require('http')
const server = http.createServer((req, res) =>{
    ...
})

server.listen(3000)
```

That is, we have to take care of importing *http*, *fs*, other packages, and also the *request* and *response* object. But with Express, we achieve the same with:

```
const express = require('express') // require express module
const app = express() // calls express function to start new Express app
app.listen(3000,()=>{
    console.log("App listening on port 3000")
})
```

Express takes care of the *http*, *request* and *response* objects behind the scenes. The callback function provided in the 2nd argument in *app.listen()* is executed when the server starts listening.

Running your App

Copy the above Express code into *index.js*, run *node index.js* in the command and see the log "App listening on port 3000" printed. We will read more about the advantages of using Express in the next section.

Handing Requests with Express

Express allows greater flexibility in responding to browser 'get' or 'post' requests. We illustrate this in the following code in **bold**:

```
const express = require('express')
```

```
const app = express()

app.listen(3000,()=>{
    console.log("App listening on port 3000")
})

app.get('/',(req,res)=>{
    res.json({
        name: 'Greg Lim'
    })
})
```

In the above code, you can see that Express has populated more operations for us to respond better to browser requests. For example, we return a JSON respond back to the browser with *res.json*. This thus lets us build APIs with Node. We can define specific routes and its response our server gives when a route is hit, for example:

```
app.get('/about',(req,res)=>{
    res.json({
        name: 'Greg Lim'
    })
})
```

This is also called *Routing* where we map requests to specific handlers depending on their URL. Previously without Express, we had to respond to individual routes with an extended *if-else* statement in one big request handler:

```
const server = http.createServer((req, res) =>{
    if(req.url === '/about')
        res.end(aboutPage)
    else if(req.url === '/contact')
        res.end(contactPage)
    else if(req.url === '/')
        res.end(homePage)
    else {
        res.writeHead(404)
        res.end(notFoundPage)
    }
})
```

With Express, we can refactor one big request handler function into many smaller request handlers that each handle a specific function. This allows us to build our app in a more modular and maintainable way.

We can also define the type of response the server serves. For example, to serve HTML files with express, we add the following:

```
const path = require('path')
...
app.get('/',(req,res)=>{
    res.sendFile(path.resolve(__dirname,'index.html'))
})
```

Code Explanation

```
const path = require('path')
```

We introduce a new module called *path*. *path* is another built in module in Node. It helps us get the specific path to the file, because if we do *res.sendFile('index.html')*, there will be error thrown as an absolute path is needed.

`path.resolve(__dirname,'index.html')` helps us get the full absolute path which otherwise changes based on different Operating Systems. For example, on Mac and Linux, we refer to a directory using */directory*, but on Windows, we refer to it using *\directory*. The *path* module ensures that things run smoothly regardless if the OS is Windows, Mac or Linux.

```
app.get('/',(req,res)=>{
    res.sendFile(path.resolve(__dirname,'index.html'))
})
```

Express also adds things like the *sendFile* method which if we had to implement without Express, would be about 45 lines of complicated file code. Thus, I hope you come to slowly appreciate how Express makes it easier to write these request handler functions and in general simplify development in Node.

Asynchronous with Call Back Functions

We have been seeing a few examples of code with callback functions. Callback functions are an important aspect in Node.js that help support tasks to be done asynchronously. That is, rather than waiting for one task to complete before executing another e.g. in PHP:

```
Task 1 -> Task 2 -> Task 3 -> Task 4 -> Completion
```

Node.js allows the possibility to performs tasks in parallel, where no task is blocking another.

```
Task 1 ->
Task 2 ->
Task 3 ->
Task 4 ->
```

How Node.js supports asynchronous code is with callback functions. For example, the below request handlers do not have to be executed synchronously.

```
app.get('/',(req,res)=>{
    // query database
})

app.get('/about',(req,res)=>{
    res.sendFile(path.resolve(__dirname,'about.html'))
})
```

That is, if a request for '/' and '/about' comes in together, it doesn't have to be the case that one request has to be completed before serving the other. Both tasks can begin at the same time. It can be that the task to query the database starts and while the database is thinking, the second request for 'about.html' can be responded. Our code is not doing two things at once, but when a task is waiting on something, the other task can execute. Asynchronous code like callback functions thus execute much faster.

Serving Other HTML files

To serve the *about* and *contact* HTML files, add the following:

```
app.get('/about',(req,res)=>{   // called when request to /about comes in
    res.sendFile(path.resolve(__dirname,'about.html'))
})

app.get('/contact',(req,res)=>{ //called when request to /contact comes
    res.sendFile(path.resolve(__dirname,'contact.html'))
```

```
})
```

If you restart the server, our app will serve the *about* file when a request to /*about* comes in and serve the *contact* file when a request to /*contact* comes in.

Note here that we use *app.get* to handle HTTP GET requests which are the most common HTTP method. GET request as its name suggest gets resources like a homepage, an image etc. GET methods do not change the state of our app, it simply retrieves. Other methods like POST and PUT do that and we will cover them in the course of this book.

Serving Static Files with Express

Now that we are serving HTML pages from our server, how do we include static files like fonts, images and CSS with Express?

To do so, in *index.js* add the line in **bold**:

```
const express = require('express')
const app = express()
const path = require('path')
app.use(express.static('public'))

app.listen(3000,()=>{
    console.log("App listening on port 3000")
})
```

app.use is a special function to increase functionality with Express by adding a function to our application's middleware stack. We will discuss more on middleware in a dedicated chapter later on.

express.static is a packaged shipped with Express that helps us serve static files. With *express.static('public')*, we specify that any request that ask for assets should get it from the 'public' directory.

To illustrate this, first create a folder called 'public' in our app folder. In it, create the sub-folders 'css' and 'js' (fig. 2.3). We will be referencing these two folders from our *index.html* file.

Figure 2.3

Referencing *index.css*

In the 'css' folder, create a file called *index.css* with the following code:

```
body {
    background-color: coral;
}
```

To reference *index.css* in *index.html*, add in *index.html* the following line:

```
<link rel="stylesheet" href="css/index.css">
<h1>Home Page</h1>
```

Note that when we reference *href="css/index.css"*, Express refers to */public/css/index.css*. That is, the url for the static file being served is determined by combining its url with 'public'.

Referencing *index.js*

To link to an external js file, we similarly add the below to *index.html*:

```
<script src="js/index.js"></script>
```

This assumes that there is a sub folder in *public* called *js* containing the file *index.js*.

32

Important note: the *index.js* that *index.html* refers to in this case is for the client side, not the server side *index.js*!

Summary

We learnt how to install third party custom packages using *npm*. A core custom package is Express which helps make it easier to handle requests and serve responses, thus making app development in Node easier in general. We generated the *package.json* file that maintains our project metadata particularly its dependencies in an organized manner. We also learnt how to serve static files to make CSS and JavaScript files available to the HTML client files.

CHAPTER 3: BEGINNING OUR BLOG PROJECT

Downloading the Blog Template

As this book is not about website design, CSS or how to come up with a graphical user interface, we will use a blog template to start off our project. We will be using the 'Clean Blog' theme from *startbootstrap.com* (https://startbootstrap.com/themes/clean-blog/ fig. 3.1).

Figure 3.1

Download the *.zip* file that contains the theme and extract it to a new folder for this project.

Go to Terminal and *cd* to the new folder. Run *npm init* and say 'yes' to all the questions for *package.json* to be generated for us.

Next in the folder, install Express with:

```
npm install express
```

In that folder, create *index.js* which will serve as the root of the project. Fill it with the following code:

```
const express = require('express')

const app = new express()

app.listen(4000, ()=>{
    console.log('App listening on port 4000')
})
```

As covered earlier, start the server by running *node index.js* in Terminal.

Automatic Server Restart with *nodemon*

For now, we have been starting and stopping our server each time we make a code change in *index.js*. Now, we will install a package called *nodemon* that automatically detects code changes and restart the server so we don't have to manually stop and restart it. Install *nodemon* with the following command:

```
npm install nodemon --save-dev
```

The *--save* option is to have the dependencies listed in our *package.json* so that someone else can install the dependencies later if we give them the project – they need only to run *npm install* with no arguments. You can also manually edit *package.json* and then run *npm install* to add dependencies. Without the *--save* option, we would have the *node_modules* folder but it will not be reflected in our *package.json*.

The *-dev* option is to specify that we install *nodemon* for development purposes only. We do not want *nodemon* to be part of the production version of the app. When *nodemon* is installed, in *package.json* you can see it listed under *devDependencies*. This indicates that the package is for development purposes only and not included in our app when we deploy it.

npm start

We will be starting our app from within a *npm* script with *npm start*. To do so, in *package.json*, go to "scripts" and make the following change:

```
...
"scripts": {
  "start": "nodemon index.js"
},
...
```

So instead of running our app with *node index.js* as we have done previously, we now run it with: **npm start**. *npm start* looks inside our *package.json* file, see that we have added a script called *start*, and run the associated command i.e. *nodemon index.js. nodemon* watches our files for changes and automatically restarts the server when there are code changes.

We can of course just run *nodemon index.js* directly, but because *npm start* is a convention where most Node web servers can be started with *npm start*. That is to say, we don't have to know the actual file name whether *index.js* or *app.js*, we just start the server with *npm start*.

Also, *npm start* allows you to run more complex command(s) when your app grows e.g. starting database server or clearing log files before starting up the server. Now, make sure that the server is running with *npm start*.

public folder for serving static files

Next, we will register a *public* folder for our static files as what we have done in the previous chapter. In *index.js*, add the following:

```
const express = require('express')

const app = new express()
app.use(express.static('public'))

app.listen(4000, ()=>{
    console.log('App listening on port 4000')
})
```

With this, Express will expect all static assets to be in the *public* directory. Thus, proceed to create a new folder called *public* in the app directory. Move the following files from the downloaded template files into *public*:

```
index.html
about.html
contact.html
post.html
```

Next, move the following downloaded template folders into *public*:

```
css
img
js
vendor
```

If you are wondering how to know which files and folders to move to *public*, look inside *index.html* and see which static assets it is referencing. I go through the relevant pieces of *index.html* below:

In the head tag *index.html*, we can see that it is referencing folders *vendor* and *css*.

```html
<head>
  ...
  <title>Clean Blog - Start Bootstrap Theme</title>

  <!-- Bootstrap core CSS -->
  <link href="vendor/bootstrap/css/bootstrap.min.css" rel="stylesheet">

  <!-- Custom fonts for this template -->
  <link href="vendor/fontawesome-free/css/all.min.css" rel="stylesheet"
type="text/css">
    ...

  <!-- Custom styles for this template -->
  <link href="css/clean-blog.min.css" rel="stylesheet">

</head>
```

In *body*, under the navigation bar, we see that it refers to *index.html*, *about.html*, *post.html* and *contact.html*. These therefore are to be in *public* root.

```html
<body>
  <!-- Navigation -->
  <nav class="navbar navbar-expand-lg navbar-light fixed-top" id="mainNav">
    <div class="container">
        ...
      <div class="collapse navbar-collapse" id="navbarResponsive">
        <ul class="navbar-nav ml-auto">
          <li class="nav-item">
            <a class="nav-link" href="index.html">Home</a>
          </li>
          <li class="nav-item">
            <a class="nav-link" href="about.html">About</a>
          </li>
          <li class="nav-item">
            <a class="nav-link" href="post.html">Sample Post</a>
          </li>
          <li class="nav-item">
            <a class="nav-link" href="contact.html">Contact</a>
          </li>
        </ul>
      </div>
    </div>
  </nav>
```

Towards the end of the file, *vendor* is again referenced. *js* is also referenced.

```html
  <!-- Bootstrap core JavaScript -->
  <script src="vendor/jquery/jquery.min.js"></script>
  <script src="vendor/bootstrap/js/bootstrap.bundle.min.js"></script>

  <!-- Custom scripts for this template -->
  <script src="js/clean-blog.min.js"></script>

</body>
</html>
```

And that is why we move `index.html, about.html, contact.html, post.html` template files and `css, img, js, vendor` template folders into *public*.

Now if you go to localhost:4000, Express should serve your *index.html* along with its static assets (fig. 3.1).

Figure 3.1

And if you click the *about*, *sample post* and *contact* links, it should navigate to those pages as well.

Creating Page Routes

Currently, we are serving *index.html*, *about.html*, *post.html* and *contact.html* from the *public* folder, which is treating it like any other static file. We should however be serving these files by defining specific routes with *app.get* and responding when specific routes are hit as what we have done before. To do so, create a *pages* folder in the root app directory and move all the HTML files from *public* over there.

After copying the files, we will setup the routes for the various pages. To setup the homepage route, we register a *get* route to serve the home HTML when we receive a request from the browser. Add the following in *index.js*:

```
const express = require('express')
const path = require('path')

const app = new express()
...

app.get('/',(req,res)=>{
    res.sendFile(path.resolve(__dirname, 'pages/index.html'))
})
```

Now when a request is made to the home page route '/', *index.html* will be served.

Try it Yourself

Can you try creating the *about, sample post* and *contact page* routes on your own? The route code should be similar to what we have created for our home page route. So, take some time and try it on your own. Else, you can follow my solution below.

In *index.js*, create the new route for *about, contact* and *sample* by adding the below:

```
app.get('/about',(req,res)=>{
    res.sendFile(path.resolve(__dirname,'pages/about.html'))
})

app.get('/contact',(req,res)=>{
    res.sendFile(path.resolve(__dirname,'pages/contact.html'))
})

app.get('/post',(req,res)=>{
    res.sendFile(path.resolve(__dirname,'pages/post.html'))
})
```

Do note that we have to append 'pages/' before the html file because we are storing the HTML files in the *pages* folder.

Links in *index.html*

Now if you run your app and try to navigate to about, contact and sample post pages from the nav bar, you will realize that they don't work or get a "Cannot GET /contact.html" error. This is because in *index.html*, we currently refer to other pages with *href* links to the actual html files i.e. *about.html* as shown below:

```
<li class="nav-item">
  <a class="nav-link" href="index.html">Home</a>
</li>
<li class="nav-item">
  <a class="nav-link" href="about.html">About</a>
</li>
```

```
<li class="nav-item">
  <a class="nav-link" href="post.html">Sample Post</a>
</li>
<li class="nav-item">
  <a class="nav-link" href="contact.html">Contact</a>
</li>
```

Because we have already moved them away from the *public* folder, they can't be found. Instead we have to use the routes that we defined earlier to navigate to those pages. That is, in *index.html*, replace the href links with the below routes:

```
<li class="nav-item">
  <a class="nav-link" href="/">Home</a>
</li>
<li class="nav-item">
  <a class="nav-link" href="/about">About</a>
</li>
<li class="nav-item">
  <a class="nav-link" href="/post">Sample Post</a>
</li>
<li class="nav-item">
  <a class="nav-link" href="/contact">Contact</a>
</li>
```

We have to repeat the above link change for the nav bar in *about.html*, *contact.html* and *post.html* as well, else the links will still break. You will quickly realize that this is tedious, repetitive work. What if we have to add a new link to our nav bar? That means we have to repeat the same code for the nav bar in all of our pages. You will realize that this is very unnecessary duplicative work! It is not scalable and it becomes increasingly difficult as our app grows.

In this next section, we will resolve this problem by using templating engines.

Summary

We began our blog project with an existing blog template from *startbootstrap.com* and incorporated it into a Node.js project. Using the *nodemon* package, we automatically detect code changes in our project and restart the server. Page routes were created to serve the *home*, *about* and *post* pages. A navigation bar was created to contain the links to these routes.

Refer to https://github.com/greglim81/express_chap3-8 for the source code of this chapter.

Chapter 4: Templating Engines

Templating engines help us dynamically render HTML pages in contrast to just having fixed static pages which in the earlier chapter gives us a problem that we have to duplicate the nav bar code for all static pages. In this chapter, we will refactor our app to use a templating engine that allows us to abstract our app into different layout files so that we don't repeat common code, yet still serve the same HTML file as before.

There are many templating engines out there like Handlebars, Pug, and more. But we will use 'EJS' (which stands for Embedded JavaScript) because it is one of the more popular templating engines and is made by the people who created Express. All these different templating engines at the end of the day have the same purpose which is to output HTML.

As stated on its site, EJS is a simple templating language that lets us generate HTML with plain JavaScript in simple straightforward scriplet tags i.e. <%= ... %>.

First, install EJS with *npm*:

```
npm install ejs --save
```

To use EJS in our app, in *index.js* add the following:

```
const express = require('express')
const path = require('path')

const app = new express()
const ejs = require('ejs')
app.set('view engine','ejs')
```

With *app.set('view engine','ejs')*, we tell Express to use EJS as our templating engine, that any file ending in *.ejs* should be rendered with the EJS package.

Previously, we responded to a *get* request with the following:

```
app.get('/',(req,res)=>{
    res.sendFile(path.resolve(__dirname,'pages/index.html'))
})
```

Now with EJS, we do the following,

```
app.get('/',(req,res)=>{
    res.render('index');
})
```

We send a view to the user by using *res.render()*. Express adds the *render* method to the *response* object. **res.render('index') will look in a 'views' folder for the file index.ejs.** Thus, we rename our current *pages* folder to *views*. And in it, rename the file extension of *index.html* to *index.ejs*.

We also change the *get* request handlers with *res.render* for *about, contact* and *post* routes:

```
app.get('/about',(req,res)=>{
    //res.sendFile(path.resolve(__dirname,'pages/about.html'))
    res.render('about');
})
app.get('/contact',(req,res)=>{
    //res.sendFile(path.resolve(__dirname,'pages/contact.html'))
    res.render('contact');
})
app.get('/post',(req,res)=>{
    //res.sendFile(path.resolve(__dirname,'pages/post.html'))
    res.render('post')
})
```

Thus, change the file extensions of *about.html, contact.html,* and *post.html* to *about.ejs, contact.ejs* and *post.ejs*. In all, we should now have a *views* folder with the following EJS files (fig. 4.1).

Figure 4.1

Layouts

To solve the problem of repetitive code (e.g. nav bar, footer) appearing in each page, we will use the concept of a layout file. A layout file contains everything common in a page, for e.g., navbar layout, header layout, footer layout, scripts layout. Each page will then include these layout files in additional to their own content. This results in a much concise, readable and manageable file.

In *index.ejs*, notice the repeating elements that is, the <head>, <nav>, <footer> and <script> elements that also appear in the other views. Our aim is to extract these portion of common HTML code into their own separate layout files i.e. *header.ejs*, *navbar.ejs*, *footer.ejs* and *scripts.ejs*. We then just *include* the files that need them instead of repeating the entire code thus reducing much code clutter.

First, create a sub folder in *views* called *layouts* to store these files.

Next, extract the <head> HTML into *header.ejs* as shown below:

```
<head>

    <meta charset="utf-8">
    <meta name="viewport" content="width=device-width, initial-scale=1, shrink-
to-fit=no">
    <meta name="description" content="">
    <meta name="author" content="">

    <title>Clean Blog - Start Bootstrap Theme</title>
```

```
<!-- Bootstrap core CSS -->
<link href="vendor/bootstrap/css/bootstrap.min.css" rel="stylesheet">

<!-- Custom fonts for this template -->
<link href="vendor/fontawesome-free/css/all.min.css" rel="stylesheet"
type="text/css">
<link
href='https://fonts.googleapis.com/css?family=Lora:400,700,400italic,700italic'
rel='stylesheet' type='text/css'>
<link
href='https://fonts.googleapis.com/css?family=Open+Sans:300italic,400italic,600it
alic,700italic,800italic,400,300,600,700,800' rel='stylesheet' type='text/css'>

<!-- Custom styles for this template -->
<link href="css/clean-blog.min.css" rel="stylesheet">

</head>
```

Next, extract the <nav> HTML into layout file *navbar.ejs*:

```
<!-- Navigation -->
<nav class="navbar navbar-expand-lg navbar-light fixed-top" id="mainNav">
  <div class="container">
    <a class="navbar-brand" href="index.html">Start Bootstrap</a>
    <button class="navbar-toggler navbar-toggler-right" type="button" data-
toggle="collapse" data-target="#navbarResponsive" aria-
controls="navbarResponsive" aria-expanded="false" aria-label="Toggle navigation">
      Menu
      <i class="fas fa-bars"></i>
    </button>
    <div class="collapse navbar-collapse" id="navbarResponsive">
      <ul class="navbar-nav ml-auto">
        <li class="nav-item">
          <a class="nav-link" href="/">Home</a>
        </li>
        <li class="nav-item">
          <a class="nav-link" href="/about">About</a>
        </li>
        <li class="nav-item">
          <a class="nav-link" href="/post">Sample Post</a>
        </li>
        <li class="nav-item">
          <a class="nav-link" href="/contact">Contact</a>
        </li>
      </ul>
    </div>
```

```
        </div>
    </nav>
```

Extract the <footer> HTML into layout file *footer.ejs*:

```html
<!-- Footer -->
<footer>
    <div class="container">
        <div class="row">
        <div class="col-lg-8 col-md-10 mx-auto">
            <ul class="list-inline text-center">
            <li class="list-inline-item">
                <a href="#">
                <span class="fa-stack fa-lg">
                    <i class="fas fa-circle fa-stack-2x"></i>
                    <i class="fab fa-twitter fa-stack-1x fa-inverse"></i>
                </span>
                </a>
            </li>
            <li class="list-inline-item">
                <a href="#">
                <span class="fa-stack fa-lg">
                    <i class="fas fa-circle fa-stack-2x"></i>
                    <i class="fab fa-facebook-f fa-stack-1x fa-inverse"></i>
                </span>
                </a>
            </li>
            <li class="list-inline-item">
                <a href="#">
                <span class="fa-stack fa-lg">
                    <i class="fas fa-circle fa-stack-2x"></i>
                    <i class="fab fa-github fa-stack-1x fa-inverse"></i>
                </span>
                </a>
            </li>
            </ul>
            <p class="copyright text-muted">Copyright &copy; Your Website
2019</p>
        </div>
        </div>
    </div>
</footer>
```

And finally extract the <script> elements into *scripts.ejs*.

```
<!-- Bootstrap core JavaScript -->
<script src="vendor/jquery/jquery.min.js"></script>
<script src="vendor/bootstrap/js/bootstrap.bundle.min.js"></script>

<!-- Contact Form JavaScript -->
<script src="js/jqBootstrapValidation.js"></script>
<script src="js/contact_me.js"></script>

<!-- Custom scripts for this template -->
<script src="js/clean-blog.min.js"></script>
```

Having extracted header, nav, footer and scripts into the various layout files, *index.ejs* now *include* the various layout files in place of the extracted code as shown:

```
<!DOCTYPE html>
<html lang="en">

<%- include('layouts/header'); -%>

<body>
  <%- include('layouts/navbar'); -%>
  <!-- Page Header -->
  <header class="masthead" style="background-image: url('img/home-bg.jpg')">
    <div class="overlay"></div>
    <div class="container">
      <div class="row">
        <div class="col-lg-8 col-md-10 mx-auto">
          <div class="site-heading">
            <h1>Clean Blog</h1>
            <span class="subheading">A Blog Theme by Start Bootstrap</span>
          </div>
        </div>
      </div>
    </div>
  </header>

  <!-- Main Content -->
  …
  <hr>

  <%- include('layouts/footer'); -%>
  <%- include('layouts/scripts'); -%>

</body>
</html>
```

Code Explanation

```
<%- include('layouts/header'); -%>
```

The *include* call receives a path relative to the template. So, since the path of *header.ejs* is in *./views/layouts/header.ejs* and *index.ejs* is in *./views/index.ejs*, we specify *include('layouts/header')*.

We use the raw output tag *<%-* with *include* to allow rendering of the HTML output. To see the complete list of available tags in EJS, refer to its documentation in https://ejs.co/#docs under 'Tags'.

So, we have extracted the portion of common HTML code into its own layout file i.e. header, navbar, footer, scripts. Now, we can just use the *include* statement in *index.ejs*, *about.ejs*, *contact.ejs* and *post.ejs* thereby reducing much repetitive code.

about, contact and post.ejs files

So, proceed to do the same for *about.ejs*, *contact.ejs* and *post.ejs* files as what we have done for *index.ejs*. Notice how trimmed our files are now! If you run the app, everything should run fine as the same as before.

Now if you want to change the title, just go to *views/layouts/header.ejs* and change it:

```
<head>
    ...

    <title>Super Clean Blog - Start Bootstrap Theme</title>
    ...
```

and it will be reflected in all the pages. Or if I want to add or edit a link on the navbar, just go to *views/layouts/navbar.ejs* and change it.

We have now refactored our app to use a templating engine. Templating engines allows us to abstract our app into different layout files so that we don't repeat common code, yet still serve the same HTML file as before. We will later see what more templating engines can do especially to generate dynamic content as we build our project further.

Summary

We refactored our code to use the EJS templating engine to dynamically render HTML pages. We called *res.render* to dynamically render a view with some variables. To resolve the problem of repeating code in multiple pages for e.g. navigation bar, we used EJS *layouts*.

Refer to https://github.com/greglim81/express_chap3-8 for the source code of this chapter.

CHAPTER 5: INTRODUCTION TO MONGODB

We will use MongoDB as the backend database for our app. You can of course use other solutions to persist your application data e.g. in files, in a relational SQL database, or in another kind of storage mechanism. In this chapter, we will cover the popular MongoDB for database storage.

MongoDB is a NoSQL database. Before we talk about what is a NoSQL database, let's first talk about relational databases so that we can provide a meaningful contrast. If you have not heard of a relational database before, you can think of relational databases like spreadsheets where data is structured and each entry is generally a row in a table. Relational databases are generally controlled with SQL or Structured Query Language. Examples of popular relational databases are MySQL, SQL Server and PostgreSQL.

NoSQL databases are often called non-relational databases, where NoSQL means anything that isn't an SQL (see how it infers the popularity of SQL?). It might seem like NoSQL is a protest over SQL but it actually refers to a database not structured like a spreadsheet, i.e. less rigid than SQL databases.

So, why use Mongo? Firstly, it is popular and that means there is plenty of help online, Secondly, it is mature being around since 2007 and used by companies like eBay, Craigslist and Orange.

Architecture of MongoDB

As mentioned, the architecture of MongoDB is a NoSQL database which stores information in the form of *collections* and *documents*. MongoDB stores one or more *collections*. A *collection* represents a single entity in our app, for example in an e-commerce app, we need entities like categories, users, products. Each of these entity will be a single *collection* in our database.

A *collection* then contain *documents*. A *document* is an instance of the entity containing the various relevant fields to represent the *document*. For example, a product *document* will contain name, image and price fields. Each field is a key-value pair. Documents look a lot like JSON objects with various properties (though they are technically Binary JSON or BSON). An example of a collection-document tree is shown below:

```
Database
  → Products collection
      → Product document
            {
                price: 26,
                title: "Learning Node",
                description: "Top Notch Development book",
                expiry date: 27-3-2020
            }
      → Product document
      ...
  → Users collection
      → User document
            {
                username: "123xyz",
                contact:
                    {
                        phone: "123-456-7890",
                        email: "xyz@example.com"
                    }
            }
      → User document
      ...
```

Installing MongoDB

There are a couple of ways to install MongoDB. If you Google 'install mongodb', you will be introduced various methods of installation. You can choose your preferred one. In this book, I am installing it using *brew* to install the MongoDB Community Edition on MacOS system (https://docs.mongodb.com/manual/tutorial/install-mongodb-on-os-x/). You will notice that MongoDB frequently recommends us to use its cloud-based service MongoDB Atlas. We won't use that for now, as we want to familiarize running MongoDB on our own server. But later, we will use MongoDB Atlas when we want to deploy our app to make it available to the world.

So first run:

```
brew tap mongodb/brew
```

to tap the official MongoDB formula repository.

Next, run (we will be using version 4.0 in this book):

```
brew install mongodb-community@4.0
```

In addition to the binaries, the install creates:

the configuration file (/usr/local/etc/mongod.conf)

Running MongoDB

To run MongoDB (i.e. the *mongod* process) in the foreground, run the following:

```
mongod --config /opt/homebrew/etc/mongod.conf
```

Installing MongoDB Compass

Next, we will install MongoDB Compass which is a client tool provided by the MongoDB team itself to help us see our database visually. So, either *google* MongoDB Compass or go to https://www.mongodb.com/download-center/compass to download and install it. Installation should be straightforward.

Mongoose

To talk to MongoDB from Node, we need a library. Mongoose is an officially supported Node.js package (https://www.npmjs.com/package/mongoose) that helps us do this. To install, run

```
npm install mongoose
```

Connecting to MongoDB from Node

First in *index.js*, add the following code:

```
const mongoose = require('mongoose');
mongoose.connect('mongodb://localhost/my_database', {useNewUrlParser:
true}
```

We define a connection with *mongoose.connect* which takes in the parameter host and database name. In our case, because our database is running on the local machine, we use *localhost*. We also specify the name of the database we want to connect to, in our case *my_database*. While connecting, MongoDB will automatically create this database for us if it does not exist.

Defining a Model

Now, in your app directory, create a directory called *models*. This folder will contain *models* which are objects that represent collections in our database. In it, we create our first model file called *BlogPost.js* with the following code:

```
const mongoose = require('mongoose')
const Schema = mongoose.Schema;

const BlogPostSchema = new Schema({
  title: String,
  body: String
});
```

Models are defined through the *Schema* interface. Remember that a *collection* represents an entity in our app. e.g. users, products, blogposts. A *schema* represents how a collection looks like. This means that each *document* in the *collection* would have the fields specified in the *schema*.

Still in *BlogPost.js*, continue adding the following code:

```
...
const BlogPost = mongoose.model('BlogPost',BlogPostSchema);

module.exports = BlogPost
```

We access the database via *mongoose.model*. The first argument is the singular name of the collection your model is for. Mongoose automatically looks for the plural version of your model name. In our case, because we use *BlogPost*, Mongoose will create the model for our *BlogPosts* collection, not *BlogPost* collection.

Lastly, we export the *BlogPost* variable so that when other files require this file, they know to grab *BlogPost*. Note that you can export only one variable.

CRUD Operations with Mongoose Models

Having established the connection to MongoDB, we next illustrate CRUD (create, read, update, delete) operations via Mongoose. For sake of simplicity, we will illustrate CRUD in a separate test file to understand the concepts before applying them to our project.

In your app directory, create a file *test.js* with the following code:

```
const mongoose = require('mongoose')

const BlogPost = require('./models/BlogPost')

mongoose.connect('mongodb://localhost/my_database', {useNewUrlParser:
true});

BlogPost.create({
    title: 'The Mythbuster Guide to Saving Money on Energy Bills',
    body: 'If you have been here a long time, you might remember when I
went on ITV Tonight to dispense a masterclass in saving money on energy
bills. Energy-saving is one of my favourite money topics, because once
you get past the boring bullet-point lists, a whole new world of thrifty
nerdery opens up. You know those bullet-point lists. You start spotting
them everything at this time of year. They go like this:'
}, (error, blogpost) =>{
    console.log(error,blogpost)
})
```

Code Explanation

```
const BlogPost = require('./models/BlogPost')
```

We import the *BlogPost* model we just created by specifying its relative path. *BlogPost* represents the *BlogPosts* collection in the database.

```
mongoose.connect('mongodb://localhost/my_database', {useNewUrlParser: true});
```

We then proceed to connect to the database. Remember that if *my_database* doesn't exist, it will be created for us.

```
BlogPost.create({
    title: 'The Mythbuster Guide to Saving Money on Energy Bills',
    body: 'If you have been here a long time, you might remember when I
went on ITV Tonight to dispense a masterclass in saving money on energy
bills. Energy-saving is one of my favourite money topics…'
}, (error, blogpost) =>{
    console.log(error, blogpost)
})
```

We then create a new *BlogPost* document in our database with a function in *BlogPost* called *create*. In the first argument, we pass in the data for the blogpost document. In the 2nd argument, we pass in a call back function which is called when *create* finishes execution. Mongoose gives us any error in the *error* argument if there was any during the *create* operation. It also return us the newly created post in the *blogpost* argument.

To execute *test.js*, run *node test.js* in the Terminal. You should see *null* (error) and the *blogpost* object being logged like the below:

```
null { _id: 5cb436980b33147489eadfbb,
   title: 'The Mythbuster Guide to Saving Money on Energy Bills',
   body:
    'If you have been here a long time, you might remember when I went on
ITV Tonight to dispense a masterclass in saving money on energy bills.
Energy-saving is one of my favourite money topics, because once you get
past the boring bullet-point lists, a whole new world of thrifty nerdery
opens up. You know those bullet-point lists. You start spotting them
everything at this time of year. They go like this:',
   __v: 0 }
```

Notice that there is an additional field *_id*. *_id* is a unique id provided by MongoDB for every document.

Visualizing Data in MongoDB

To see the data visually in MongoDB, open up MongoDB Compass and you should see *my_database* on the left panel (fig. 5.1). Under it, you should see the collection *blogposts*.

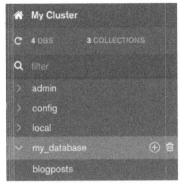

Figure 5.1

And if you click on *blogposts*, you will be able to see the *blogpost* document that we have just created (fig. 5.2). Try inserting more blog posts and see them reflected in MongoDB.

Figure 5.2

Reading Data from MongoDB using Mongoose

To select all documents in *BlogPosts* collection: pass an empty document as the query filter parameter to the first argument of the *find* method.

```
BlogPost.find({}, (error, blogspot) =>{
    console.log(error,blogspot)
})
```

The query filter parameter determines the select criteria. Thus, to find all documents in *BlogPosts* collection with a particular title for e.g. `'The Mythbuster's Guide to Saving Money on Energy Bills'`, we do:

```
BlogPost.find({
    title:'The Mythbuster's Guide to Saving Money on Energy Bills'
}, (error, blogspot) =>{
    console.log(error,blogspot)
})
```

Or, to find all documents in *BlogPosts* collection with 'The' in the title, we do:

```
BlogPost.find({
    title:/The/}, (error, blogspot) =>{
    console.log(error,blogspot)
})
```

That is, we place the wildcard operator before and after *The*. For those familiar with SQL, '/' acts like '%'.

To get single database documents, i.e. to retrieve single documents with unique id *_id*, we use the *findById* method:

```
var id = "5cb436980b33147489eadfbb";

BlogPost.findById(id, (error, blogspot) =>{
    console.log(error,blogspot)
})
```

There are many other search constraints conditions you can apply to *find*. Refer to https://docs.mongodb.com/manual/tutorial/query-documents/ for more information.

Updating Records

To update a record, we use *findByIdAndUpdate* where we provide *id* as the first argument and the fields/values to be updated in the second argument.

```
var id = "5cb436980b33147489eadfbb";
```

```
BlogPost.findByIdAndUpdate(id,{
    title:'Updated title'
}, (error, blogspot) =>{
    console.log(error,blogspot)
})
```

Deleting Single Record

To delete a record, we use the *findByIdAndDelete* where we provide *id* as the first argument.

```
var id = "5cb436980b33147489eadfbb";

BlogPost.findByIdAndDelete(id, (error, blogspot) =>{
    console.log(error,blogspot)
})
```

Summary

We were introduced to MongoDB, a NoSQL database that stores data in the form of collections and documents. Using Mongoose, we connected our Node application with the Mongo database. We defined models using the *schema* interface to represent the collections in our database. We illustrated Create, Read, Update and Delete operations via Mongoose. Finally, we used MongoDB Compass to see the stored data visually in MongoDB.

Refer to https://github.com/greglim81/express_chap3-8 for the source code of this chapter.

CHAPTER 6: APPLYING MONGODB TO OUR PROJECT

Having introduced MongoDB, we now use MongoDB database to build our app. First, we will implement the functionality for users to create a new post. For that, we will need a view for users to input the data.

In the *views* folder, create a new file *create.ejs*. As a starting point, copy the code from *contact.ejs* into *create.ejs*. That is, *create.ejs* like the other views will include the header, navbar, footer and scripts. But change the *<h1>* text to 'Create New Post':

Next, register the route for 'Create New Post' by appending the below to *index.js*:

```
app.get('/posts/new',(req,res)=>{
    res.render('create')
}
```

Next, add the 'New Post' in the nav bar. In *views/layouts/navbar.ejs*, add the following:

```
<div class="collapse navbar-collapse" id="navbarResponsive">
<ul class="navbar-nav ml-auto">
  <li class="nav-item">
    <a class="nav-link" href="/">Home</a>
  </li>
  <li class="nav-item">
    <a class="nav-link" href="/about">About</a>
  </li>
  <li class="nav-item">
    <a class="nav-link" href="/post">Sample Post</a>
  </li>
  <li class="nav-item">
    <a class="nav-link" href="/contact">Contact</a>
  </li>
  <li class="nav-item">
      <a class="nav-link" href="/posts/new">New Post</a>
  </li>
</ul>
```

```
</div>
```

Now if you run your app and go to your 'New Post' view, the page should appear but it seems that it could not reference the static files like *css*, *images*, *js* and *vendor* folders (fig. 6.1).

Figure 6.1

This is because our page is a two-level route and can't reference the required static files for e.g. in *header.ejs*, because the *href* is:

```
<!-- Bootstrap core CSS -->
<link href="vendor/bootstrap/css/bootstrap.min.css" rel="stylesheet">
```

It cannot find a *vendor* folder at its sub level. To rectify this, we need *href* to point to an absolute reference by simply adding a '/' before it:

```
<link href="/vendor/bootstrap/css/bootstrap.min.css" rel="stylesheet">
```

Thus, go back to *header.ejs, scripts.ejs* and *create.ejs* to make sure that *hrefs* are absolute references. i.e. in *header.ejs*:

```
<head>

    ...

    <title>Super Clean Blog - Start Bootstrap Theme</title>

    <!-- Bootstrap core CSS -->
    <link href="/vendor/bootstrap/css/bootstrap.min.css" rel="stylesheet">

    <!-- Custom fonts for this template -->
    <link href="/vendor/fontawesome-free/css/all.min.css" rel="stylesheet"
type="text/css">
    ...

    <!-- Custom styles for this template -->
    <link href="/css/clean-blog.min.css" rel="stylesheet">

</head>
```

In *scripts.ejs*:

```
  <!-- Bootstrap core JavaScript -->
  <script src="/vendor/jquery/jquery.min.js"></script>
  <script src="/vendor/bootstrap/js/bootstrap.bundle.min.js"></script>

  <!-- Contact Form JavaScript -->
  <script src="/js/jqBootstrapValidation.js"></script>
  <script src="/js/contact_me.js"></script>

  <!-- Custom scripts for this template -->
  <script src="/js/clean-blog.min.js"></script>
```

In *create.ejs*:

```
<!DOCTYPE html>
<html lang="en">

<%- include('layouts/header'); -%>

<body>
```

```
<%- include('layouts/navbar'); -%>

<!-- Page Header -->
<header class="masthead" style="background-image: url('/img/contact-bg.jpg')">
  ...
</header>
```

...

With this, two level (and further levels) routes can have absolute references to our static assets.

Now if you run your app, and go to your 'New Post' view, the page should appear fine as it is able to reference the static files like css, images, js and vendor folders.

In *create.ejs*, there is already an existing form from *contact.ejs*. In place of *name*, we change it to *title* (blog title). Because we do not need the email and phone number fields, remove it. And rename 'Message' to *body* (blog content body).

For simplicity's sake, we have also removed certain form validation elements like *required data-validation-required-message="Please enter a message."* and alert messages (*<p class="help-block text-danger"></p>*) as we want to focus on getting our form right. We will later come back to form validation and presenting alert messages. The create form should look something like:

...

```
<!-- Main Content -->
<div class="container"> // bootstrap classes
  <div class="row">
    <div class="col-lg-8 col-md-10 mx-auto">
      <form action="/posts/store" method="POST">
        <div class="control-group">
          <div class="form-group floating-label-form-group controls">
            <label>Title</label>
            <input type="text" class="form-control" placeholder="Title"
            id="title" name="title" >
          </div>
        </div>
        <div class="control-group">
          <div class="form-group floating-label-form-group controls">
            <label>Description</label>
            <textarea rows="5" class="form-control"
            id="body" name="body" ></textarea>
          </div>
```

```
          </div>
          <br>
          <div class="form-group">
            <button type="submit" class="btn btn-primary"
              id="sendMessageButton">Send</button>
          </div>
        </form>
      </div>
    </div>
  </div>
...
```

Note that you need the *name* attribute for each field i.e.
```
<input type="text" class="form-control" placeholder="Title" id="title"
name="title" >
```
Else, the data won't be passed from the form to the server.

Also note that in:
```
<form action="/posts/store" method="POST">
```

It means that when the form is submitted, the browser will make a 'POST' request to the */posts/store* end point. A 'POST' request is needed to pass form data from the browser to our Node.js app to create the record in the database.

In *index.js* add the following function to handle the POST request:

```
app.post('/posts/store',(req,res)=>{
    console.log(req.body)
    res.redirect('/')
})
```

In the function, we get the form data from the browser via the request *body* attribute. But to enable this, we first need to install the body parsing middleware by adding in *index.js*:

```
...
app.use(express.static('public'))
app.use(express.json())
app.use(express.urlencoded())
...
```

The body parsing middleware parse incoming request bodies in a middleware and make the form data available under the *req.body* property.

Here, we handle a POST request which is generally used to request an addition to the state of the server unlike GET where we simply get resources. A user POSTs a blog entry, a photo, signing up for an account, buying an item etc. POST is used to create records on servers. For modifying existing records, we use the PUT request.

Running our App

If you run your app now, go to 'New Post' and fill in the form and hit submit. You will be redirected to the home page with the response's *redirect* method (Express adds the *redirect* method to the *response* object for us – using just Node, redirecting will need a lot more code). In the console log, you will see your entered values in an object e.g.:

```
{ title: 'title1', body: 'body1' }
```

This is thus how we can retrieve data entered into a form. A new *body* object containing the parsed data is populated on the *request* object. You can access individual properties in the body object i.e. *req.body.title, req.body.body.*

Saving Posts to the Database

Having the browser form data in *req.body*, we now use it with the *BlogPost* model to create a new document in the *BlogPosts* collection, or in other words, have our data stored in the database. Add the following in *index.js*:

```
...
const BlogPost = require('./models/BlogPost.js')
...

app.post('/posts/store',(req,res)=>{
    // model creates a new doc with browser data
    BlogPost.create(req.body,(error,blogpost) =>{
        res.redirect('/')
    })
})
```

We import the *BlogPost* model, call its *create* method, provide *req.body* as first argument and a callback function as the 2nd argument which is called when *create* completes.

If you run your app, fill in data into the form and hit submit. You can see your newly created *blogpost* data in the *BlogPosts* collection (fig. 6.2).

Figure 6.2

You might notice that our code for creating a blog post becomes slightly more complex in that we have a callback function in a callback function. When our app grows and we make more asynchronous method calls, it might be the case that we might have more callback layers. This is what we often refer to as 'callback hell', where the nested callback code is difficult to understand.

```
app.post('/posts/store',(req,res)=>{
    // model creates a new doc with browser data
    BlogPost.create(req.body,(error,blogpost) =>{
        res.redirect('/')
    })
})
```

To resolve this, we can alternatively use a feature in ES8 called *async* and *await* for asynchronous method calling as shown in the following code:

```
app.post('/posts/store', async (req,res)=>{
    await BlogPost.create(req.body)
    res.redirect('/')
})
```

With *async*, we specify that the following method is an asynchronous call. And using *await* for *BlogPost.create*, we are saying that we will await the completion of the current line before the below line can be executed. This thus lets us have more readable code.

Displaying a List of Blog Posts

To display the list of blog posts, we use the *BlogPost* model's *find* method (we have previously went through *find* in the "Introduction to MongoDB" chapter) to find all the database records. We do this whenever the home page is requested. Thus in *app.get* for the home page i.e. '/', we do:

```
app.get('/',async (req,res)=>{
    const blogposts = await BlogPost.find({})
    res.render('index',{
        blogposts: blogposts
    });
})
```

Having retrieved all the blog posts and assigning them to the variable *blogposts*, we pass back the *blogposts* data to the client browser by providing it as the 2nd argument to *render*. And whenever the key name and value name are the same (e.g. *blogposts: blogposts*), we can shorten it to simply:

```
app.get('/',async (req,res)=>{
    const blogposts = await BlogPost.find({})
    res.render('index',{
        blogposts
    });
})
```

With this, *index.ejs* view now has access to the *blogposts* variable.

Because we console log *blogposts* with *console.log(blogposts)*, we can see that *blogposts* is an array of *BlogPost* objects.

```
[ { _id: 5cb836f610d8d629530fcf82,
    title: 'title2',
    body: 'desc2',
    __v: 0 },
  { _id: 5cb8371810d8d629530fcf83,
    title: 'title3',
    body: 'desc3',
    __v: 0 },
  { _id: 5cb839e78e235d2aa29d87e1,
    title: 'title4',
    body: 'desc4',
    __v: 0 } ]
```

Dynamic Data with Templating Engines

Now that we have the *blogposts* data returned in an array, we will use our EJS templating engine to dynamically display the blog posts in the home view.

In *index.ejs*, you currently see repeated *<div class="post-preview">* tags each representing a blog post. Thus, we will loop through the *blogposts* array in a *for* loop and render a *<div class="post-preview">* tag for each blogpost with the following in **bold**:
...

```
<body>

  <%- include('layouts/navbar'); -%>
  ...

  <!-- Main Content -->
  <div class="container">
    <div class="row">
      <div class="col-lg-8 col-md-10 mx-auto">
        <% for (var i = 0; i < blogposts.length; i++) { %>
        <div class="post-preview">
          <a href="post.html">
            <h2 class="post-title">
                <%= blogposts[i].title %>
            </h2>
            <h3 class="post-subtitle">
                <%= blogposts[i].body %>
            </h3>
          </a>
          <p class="post-meta">Posted by
            <a href="#">Start Bootstrap</a>
            on September 24, 2019</p>
        </div>
        <hr>
        <% } %>
        <!-- Pager -->
          ...
      </div>
    </div>
  </div>
  <hr>
  <%- include('layouts/footer'); -%>
  <%- include('layouts/scripts'); -%>
</body>
</html>
```

Code Explanation

```
<% for (var i = 0; i < blogposts.length; i++) { %>
```

With the provided *blogposts* array, we use a *for* loop to loop through its elements.

```
<% for (var i = 0; i < blogposts.length; i++) { %>
<div class="post-preview">
  <a href="post.html">
    <h2 class="post-title">
        <%= blogposts[i].title %>
    </h2>
    <h3 class="post-subtitle">
        <%= blogposts[i].body %>
    </h3>
  </a>
  <p class="post-meta">Posted by
    <a href="#">Start Bootstrap</a>
    on September 24, 2019</p>
</div>
<hr>
<% } %>
```

We then populate the:
- blogpost title under the *<h2 class="post-title">* tag,
- blogpost body under *<h3 class="post-subtitle">*

If you run your app now, you will see the blog posts dynamically displayed (fig. 6.3).

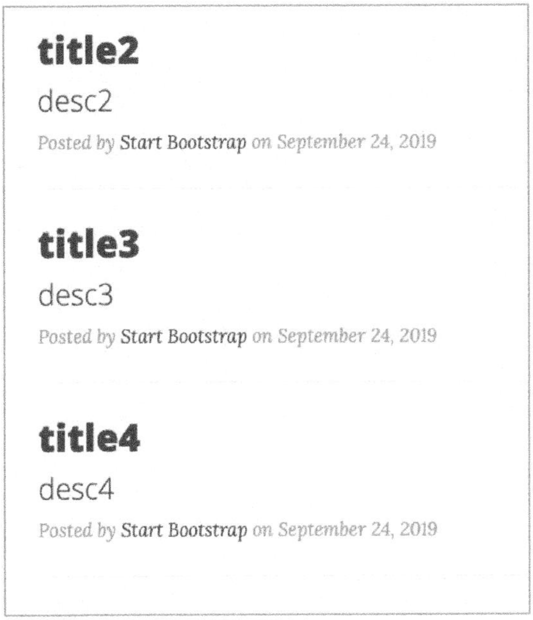

Figure 6.3

There are of course other fields that we could have populated for each blog post, for e.g.:
- individual blog post route in *<a href="post.html">*,
- blog post author name in *<p class="post-meta">Posted by <a href="#">...</a>*
- and blog post date in *on September 24, 2019</p>*

We will work to populate the blogpost author name and date in later sections of the book.

For the blogpost route, populate it as:

```
<div class="post-preview">
  <a href="/post/<%= blogposts[i]._id %>">
...
  </a>
...
</div>
```

In the next section we will work to generate single pages for each blog post route.

Try It Out

Now that we have implemented listing all blog posts in the home page, can you try as an exercise how to add a search bar and only list blog posts that fit the search terms?

71

Previously, we supplied no search criteria to *BlogPost.find({}...)* to get all the posts.

```
BlogPost.find({}, (error, blogspot) =>{
    console.log(error,blogspot)
})
```

Now, can you supply query filter parameters to determine the search criteria? E.g. to find all documents in *BlogPosts* collection with a particular title for e.g. `'The Mythbuster's Guide to Saving Money on Energy Bills'`, we do:

```
BlogPost.find({
    title:'The Mythbuster's Guide to Saving Money on Energy Bills'
}, (error, blogspot) =>{
    console.log(error,blogspot)
})
```

Or, to find all documents in BlogPosts collection with 'The' in the title, we do:

```
BlogPost.find({
    title:/The/}, (error, blogspot) =>{
    console.log(error,blogspot)
})
```

Try it out!

Single Blog Post Page

We want to display each blog post's detail in their own specific url. First we need to change the route definition for a single blog post. Currently in *index.js*, *app.get('/post...* is:

```
app.get('/post',(req,res)=>{
    res.render('post')
})
```

Change it to:

```
app.get('/post/:id',async (req,res)=>{
    const blogpost = await BlogPost.findById(req.params.id)
    res.render('post',{
        blogpost
    })
})
```

Code Explanation

```
app.get('/post/:id'…
```

First, we append a parameter to the route for a single post. *:id* represents a wild card that accepts any string value, e.g. http://localhost:4000/post/**5cb836f610d8d629530fcf82**. In our case, we have populated *id* with blogpost *_id* i.e. *<a href="/post/<%= blogposts[i]._id %>">*.

The parameters after */post/* can be retrieved with *req.params*. For example, if we run

```
app.get('/post/:id',async (req,res)=>{
    console.log(req.params)
})
```

We get the *params* object being printed out:

```
{ id: '5cb836f610d8d629530fcf82' }
```

That is, it prints out the key and value of the *param* in the route. With the param *id*, we use it to call *BlogPost.findById* which retrieves the specific blog post with that id and pass the *blogpost* variable to *post.ejs*.

```
app.get('/post/:id',async (req,res)=>{
    const blogpost = await BlogPost.findById(req.params.id)
    res.render('post',{
        blogpost
    })
})
```

post.ejs

To dynamically display each post's unique data in *post.ejs*, make the following changes in **bold**:

```
<!DOCTYPE html>
<html lang="en">
    <%- include('layouts/header'); -%>
<body>
    <%- include('layouts/navbar'); -%>
  <!-- Page Header -->
  <header class="masthead" style="background-image: url('img/post-
bg.jpg')">
    <div class="overlay"></div>
    <div class="container">
      <div class="row">
```

```
              <div class="col-lg-8 col-md-10 mx-auto">
                <div class="post-heading">
                  <h1><%= blogpost.title %></h1>
                  <h2 class="subheading"><%= blogpost.body %></h2>
                  <span class="meta">Posted by
                    <a href="#">Start Bootstrap</a>
                    on August 24, 2019</span>
                </div>
              </div>
            </div>
          </div>
      </header>

      <!-- Post Content -->
      <article>
        <div class="container">
          <div class="row">
            <div class="col-lg-8 col-md-10 mx-auto">
                <%= blogpost.body %>
          </div>
        </div>
      </article>
      <hr>
      <%- include('layouts/footer'); -%>
      <%- include('layouts/scripts'); -%>
  </body>
  </html>
```

Code Explanation

To dynamically display each post's unique data, we change the title in the <h1> tag to
<h1><%= blogpost.title %></h1>,

change subheading in <h2> to **<h2 class="subheading"><%= blogpost.body %></h2>**

and article body to **<%= blogpost.body %>.**

Running your App

Now when you run your app and click on a specific post from the Home view, the Post view will be populated with that specific blog post's data. If you click on another post, the title and body will dynamically change to that blog post's data.

Adding Fields to the Schema

Because we currently only have *title* and *body* field for our blog post, we additionally require a *username* field and a *datePosted* field to know who and when the post was created. To add the fields, add in the codes in **bold** below:

```
const mongoose = require('mongoose')
const Schema = mongoose.Schema;

const BlogPostSchema = new Schema({
  title: String,
  body: String,
  username: String,
  datePosted:{ /* can declare property type with an object like this
because we need 'default' */
    type: Date,
    default: new Date()
  }
});

const BlogPost = mongoose.model('BlogPost',BlogPostSchema);
module.exports = BlogPost
```

With the added fields, make changes in *index.ejs* and *post.ejs*.

index.ejs

```
          ...
        <p class="post-meta">Posted by
          <a href="#"><%= blogposts[i].username %></a>
          on <%= blogposts[i].datePosted.toDateString() %></p>
      </div>
      <hr>
      <% } %>
      <!-- Pager -->
      <div class="clearfix">
        <a class="btn btn-primary float-right" href="#">Older Posts
&rarr;</a>
      </div>
```

```
        </div>
      </div>
    </div>
    <hr>
    <%- include('layouts/footer'); -%>
    <%- include('layouts/scripts'); -%>
  </body>
</html>
```

post.ejs

...

```
  <!-- Page Header -->
  <header class="masthead" style="background-image: url('img/post-
bg.jpg')">
    <div class="overlay"></div>
    <div class="container">
      <div class="row">
        <div class="col-lg-8 col-md-10 mx-auto">
          <div class="post-heading">
            <h1><%= blogpost.title %></h1>
            <h2 class="subheading"><%= blogpost.body %></h2>
            <span class="meta">Posted by
              <a href="#"><%= blogpost.username %></a>
              on <%= blogpost.datePosted.toDateString() %></span>
          </div>
        </div>
      </div>
    </div>
  </header>
```

...

Now delete the records in the database and re-insert the records so that our blog post contains the additional fields. This time, *datePosted* will be auto populated. Later on, we will populate the *username* field when we implement the login function.

Summary

We used MongoDB to build our blog app. We implemented a form to create a blog post and used the *express.json()* middleware to retrieve the form field data. The *BlogPost* model was used to store the data in the database. We displayed the list of blog posts in the home page with the EJS templating engine and also displayed each blog post detail in their own individual pages.

Refer to https://github.com/greglim81/express_chap3-8 for the source code of this chapter.

CHAPTER 7: UPLOADING AN IMAGE WITH EXPRESS

In this chapter, we will explore how to upload an image for a blog post. We will install a package *express-fileupload* to help upload files in Express (https://www.npmjs.com/package/express-fileupload).

As stated in its docs, run the following to install *express-fileupload*:

```
npm install --save express-fileupload
```

Next, add a file upload field in our create post form (fig. 7.1).

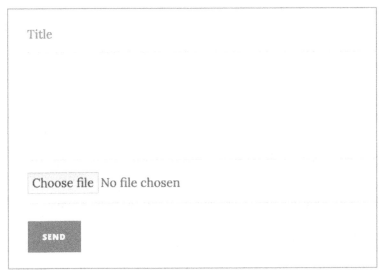

Figure 7.1

In *create.ejs*, add the following code in **bold**:

```
<form action="/posts/store" method="POST"
enctype="multipart/form-data">
   ...
  <div class="control-group">
    <div class="form-group floating-label-form-group controls">
      <label>Image</label>
```

```html
      <input type="file" class="form-control" id="image"
        name="image">
    </div>
  </div>
  <br>
  <div class="form-group">
    <button type="submit" class="btn btn-primary"
    id="sendMessageButton">Send</button>
  </div>
</form>
```

Code Explanation

```html
<form action="/posts/store" method="POST" enctype="multipart/form-data">
```

enctype="multipart/form-data" is for the browser to know that the form contains multi media. The browser will then encrypt the multi media before sending it to the server.

In *index.js*, in the request handler for '/posts/store', add:

```js
...
const fileUpload = require('express-fileupload')
app.use(fileUpload())
```

```js
...
app.post('/posts/store', (req,res)=>{
    let image = req.files.image;
    image.mv(path.resolve(__dirname,'public/img',image.name),async
      (error)=>{
        await BlogPost.create(req.body)
        res.redirect('/')
    })
})
```

Code Explanation

```js
const fileUpload = require('express-fileupload')
```

express-fileupload adds the *files* property to the *req* object so that we can access the uploaded files using *req.files*.

We then register the package in Express with *app.use(fileUpload())*

```
app.post('/posts/store', (req,res)=>{
    let image = req.files.image;
    image.mv(path.resolve(__dirname,'public/img',image.name),async
      (error)=>{
        await BlogPost.create(req.body)
        res.redirect('/')
    })
})
```

We first create a shortcut to *req.files.image* with *image*. The *req.files.image* object contains certain properties like *mv* - a function to move the file elsewhere on your server and *name*.
(See https://www.npmjs.com/package/express-fileupload for the complete list of what it contains.)

image.mv moves the uploaded file to *public/img directory* with the name from *image.name*. When this is done, we proceed to create post as what we have done before.

Do note the positioning of the *async* statement. Only in the scope where we use *await* should *async* be declared.

Running your App

When you run your app, try creating a blog post and upload an image. You should be able to see the uploaded image in *public/img* of your local directory.

Saving Uploaded Images to Database

In *BlogPost.js*, add a *image* variable of type *string* to store the file path of the image as shown:

```
...
const BlogPostSchema = new Schema({
  title: String,
  body: String,
  username: String,
  datePosted:{
    type: Date,
    default: new Date()
  },
  image: String
```

```
});
...
```

In *index.js*, specify the full *image* file path to the BlogPost *image* attribute in *create()* as shown below:

```
app.post('/posts/store', (req,res)=>{
    let image = req.files.image;
    image.mv(path.resolve(__dirname,'public/img',image.name),async
(error)=>{
        await BlogPost.create({
            ...req.body,
            image: '/img/' + image.name
        })
        res.redirect('/')
    })
})
```

When you run your app now, the new blog post will contain the image file path.

To display the image in the post view, in *post.ejs*, change the hardcoded filepath from

```
<header class="masthead" style="background-image: url('img/post-bg.jpg')">
```

to:

```
<header class="masthead" style="background-image: url('<%= blogpost.image %>')">
```

Now when you run your app and navigate to a specific blog post page with an image, it should show the image in the view (fig. 7.2).

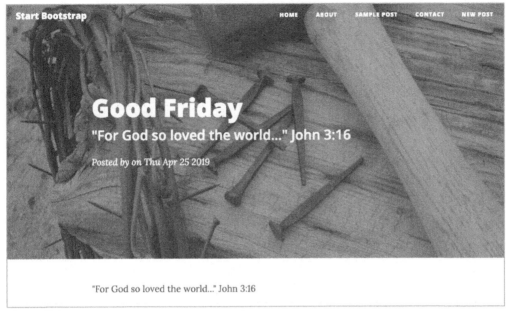

Figure 7.2

Summary

In this chapter, we explored how to upload images for each blog post and storing them in the server.

Refer to https://github.com/greglim81/express_chap3-8 for the source code of this chapter.

CHAPTER 8: INTRODUCTION TO EXPRESS MIDDLEWARE

Middleware are functions that Express executes in the middle after the incoming request which then produces an output which could either be the final output or be used by the next middleware. We can have more than one middleware and they will execute in the order they are declared. In the process, middlewares might make changes to the *request* and *response* objects.

We have actually been using middlewares. In *index.js*, when we have *app.use(...)*, we are in fact applying middlewares to Express. We have for example declared the following middlewares:

```
app.use(express.static('public'))
app.use(express.json())
app.use(express.urlencoded())
app.use(fileUpload())
```

The *use* function registers a middleware with our Express app. So, when a browser makes a request to a page for example, Express will execute all the 'use' statements sequentially before handling the request.

With *app.use(fileUpload())*, the *fileUpload* middleware modifies the *request* object and adds the *request.files* property to it. Without the *fileupload* middleware, uploading a file and retrieving it would be much more difficult!

Custom Middleware

You can even create your own custom middleware. For example, in *index.js*, add the following code to create a custom middleware:

```
...
const customMiddleWare = (req,res,next)=>{
    console.log('Custom middle ware called')
    next()
}
app.use(customMiddleWare)
...
```

Now each time you refresh your app, the message 'Custom middle ware called' will be logged in the console.

next() tells Express that the middleware is done and Express should call the next middleware function. If you remove *next()* and go to your app in the browser, the app will hang as you have not told Express to proceed on to the next middleware function. All middlewares called by *app.use* calls *next()*.

Registering Validation Middleware

A good use case of using a middleware is in form validation, where we check for the validity of form field values (field not blank etc.) Without form validation, our app currently crashes if we submit an empty new post form. We get an error *TypeError: Cannot read property 'image' of null* because the *image* property cannot be null.

With a validation middleware, Express checks to see if data filled in the fields is valid before sending the request to the server. Create the validation middleware with the below code:

```
...
const validateMiddleWare = (req,res,next)=>{
    if(req.files == null || req.body.title == null){
        return res.redirect('/posts/new')
    }
    next()
}
...
```

The `validateMiddleWare` middleware simply checks if any of the form fields are null (which means that they are not entered by the user) and if so, redirect them back to the create post page.

If we apply the middleware to our application using *app.use(validateMiddleWare)*, this middleware will be executed for all request whereas we only want it to be executed for the request to create posts. Thus, to apply middleware for specific url requests, we do:

```
...
app.use('/posts/store',validateMiddleWare)
...
```

That is, if Express sees a request from the given url '*/posts/store*', then execute the middleware *validateMiddleWare*. Note: make sure the above statement is after *app.use(fileUpload())* since we depend on the *req* object having the *files* property.

When you run your app and try to submit a create post form with the image field missing, you will be re-directed to the form page. Only when you have all fields filled in will your submission be successful.

Summary

We were introduced to middlewares in Express and how they add functionality to our application by adding features to the *request* and *respond* objects. We made use of the *validation* middleware to do form validation.

Refer to https://github.com/greglim81/express_chap3-8 for the source code of this chapter.

CHAPTER 9: REFACTORING TO MVC

Till now, we have been putting all our code into *index.js*. For example, all the request handlers *app.get*, *app.post* are in the same file. This is not the best approach when our app grows or if we are building a more complex app as *index.js* becomes too complicated and unmanageable. Thus, we will refactor our code adhering to a common pattern called the Model-View-Controller or MVC pattern.

That is, we divide our application into three interconnected parts, Model, View and Controller:
- *Model* represents the structure of the data, the format and the constraints with which it is stored. In essence, it is the database part of the application. As you might already notice, we already have that in our *models* folder currently storing the *BlogPost* model.
- *View* is what is presented to the user. Views make use of the Model and present data in a manner which the user wants. From the view, user can make changes to the data presented to them. In our app, the View consist of static or dynamic pages rendered to users. The pages are stored in a *views* folder storing various EJS files to render static and dynamic HTML websites.
- Lastly, we have *Controller* which controls the requests of the user and then generates appropriate response rendered back to the user. That is, a user interacts with the View which generates the appropriate request which is handled by the Controller which then renders the appropriate view with the Model data as a response.

We already have the Model and View layer. In this chapter, we will refactor our code to create a Controller layer by creating a *controllers* folder to store our request handlers.
So, create a new folder *controllers*, and in it create a new file *newPost.js*. This file will contain the controller handling the request from the user to create a new blog post.

In *newPost.js*, fill in the code with:

```
module.exports = (req, res) =>{
    res.render('create')
}
```

In *index.js*, we then replace the below request handler

```
app.get('/posts/new',(req,res)=>{
    res.render('create')
})
```

with:

```
const newPostController = require('./controllers/newPost')
```

...

```
app.get('/posts/new',newPostController)
```

That is, we move the existing request handler function to a separate controller file *newPost.js*. This helps to make *index.js* smaller and provide better organization by separating controller details each into their own file.

Try It Out

As an exercise, try on your own to create individual controller files for the other request handler functions.

Have you tried them? Let's go through it together now. For simplicity in our project and to allow us to focus on the essentials, we will remove the *About*, *Contact* and *Sample Post* pages since they are just standard static HTML pages.

So, in *index.js*, remove:

```
app.get('/about',(req,res)=>{
      res.render('about');
})

app.get('/contact',(req,res)=>{
      res.render('contact');
})

app.get('/post',(req,res)=>{
      res.render('post')
})
```

We would also have to remove their links from *navbar.ejs*:

```
<div class="collapse navbar-collapse" id="navbarResponsive">
  <ul class="navbar-nav ml-auto">
    <li class="nav-item">
      <a class="nav-link" href="/">Home</a>
    </li>
    <li class="nav-item">
      <a class="nav-link" href="/about">About</a>
    </li>
    <li class="nav-item">
      <a class="nav-link" href="/post">Sample Post</a>
    </li>
    <li class="nav-item">
      <a class="nav-link" href="/contact">Contact</a>
    </li>
    <li class="nav-item">
        <a class="nav-link" href="/posts/new">New Post</a>
    </li>
  </ul>
</div>
```

This leaves us to refactor the home page, store post and get individual post request handler. In *controllers* folder, create *home.js*, *storePost.js* and *getPost.js* as shown below:

home.js

```
const BlogPost = require('../models/BlogPost.js')

module.exports = async (req, res) =>{
    const blogposts = await BlogPost.find({})
    res.render('index',{
        blogposts
    });
}
```

Note that we have to import the model *BlogPost* with the *require* going up one directory (..).

getPost.js

```js
const BlogPost = require('../models/BlogPost.js')

module.exports = async (req,res)=>{
    const blogpost = await BlogPost.findById(req.params.id)
    console.log(blogpost)
    res.render('post',{
        blogpost
    });
}
```

storePost.js

```js
const BlogPost = require('../models/BlogPost.js')
const path = require('path')

module.exports = (req,res)=>{
    let image = req.files.image;
    image.mv(path.resolve(__dirname,'..','public/img',image.name),async
(error)=>{
        await BlogPost.create({
            ...req.body,
            image: '/img/' + image.name
        })
        res.redirect('/')
    })
}
```

Note that we need to import *path*. We also need to add *'..'* to *path.resolve* because we have to go up one folder before referring to *public/img*.

In *index.js*, import the following controllers we have just created:

```js
...
const homeController = require('./controllers/home')
const storePostController = require('./controllers/storePost')
const getPostController = require('./controllers/getPost')
...
```

Make the following changes to the request handlers to call the new controller functions:

```
app.get('/',homeController)
app.get('/post/:id',getPostController)
app.post('/posts/store', storePostController)
```

Because *index.js* no longer requires *path* and *BlogPost*, we can remove them.

```
const path = require('path')
const BlogPost = require('./models/BlogPost.js')
```

See how slimmer *index.js* is now and code is better organized by abstracting them to a *Controllers* layer?

Refactoring Validation Layer

We can take it further and put our validation middleware into its own folder.
Create a *middleware* directory and in it, create a new file *validationMiddleware.js*. Cut and paste the *validationMiddleware* function from *index.js* into *validationMiddleware.js* as shown below:

```
module.exports = (req,res,next)=>{
    if(req.files == null || req.body.title == null ){
        return res.redirect('/posts/new')
    }
    next()
}
```

Back in *index.js*, import the middleware with:

```
const validateMiddleware = require("./middleware/validateMiddleware");
```

And remove the previous middleware function:

```
const validateMiddleWare = (req,res,next)=>{
    if(req.files == null || req.body.title == null ){
        return res.redirect('/posts/new')
    }
    next()
}
```

If you run your app now, the form validation should take place as before. With this, we have refactored our middleware code.

In this chapter, we refactored our project code into the Model-View-Controller pattern which makes our code more manageable and organised. We particularly implemented *controllers* and abstracted code away from *index.js* preventing it from becoming messy.

Refer to https://github.com/greglim81/express_chap9 for the source code of this chapter.

CHAPTER 10: USER REGISTRATION

So far, we have been creating blog posts yet not attributing a username to them. In reality, a user should first register a user account and login before she can create blog posts. The posts then will be attributed to that user. In this chapter, we will implement user registration.

We first create the register user view. In 'views' folder, create a new file 'register.ejs'. Since we are going to have a form, we will utilize the code in *create.ejs* which already contains a form and copy its contents to *register.ejs*.

In *register.ejs*, change the header to "Register a new account"

```
...
        <div class="page-heading">
          <h1>Register a new account</h1>
        </div>
...
```

Next, change *form action* to:

```
...
<form action="/users/register" ...>
...
```

In the *title* field, change it to *username* field as shown:

```
        <div class="control-group">
          <div class="form-group floating-label-form-group controls">
            <label>User Name</label>
            <input type="text" class="form-control" placeholder="User
Name" id="username" name="username">
          </div>
        </div>
```

Delete the code for *description* since it's a textarea field. Duplicate the code for the *username* field and rename it as *password* for the *password* field as shown below. Note that *type* should be *password* to mask the characters being keyed in.

```
<div class="control-group">
  <div class="form-group floating-label-form-group controls">
    <label>Password</label>
    <input type="password" class="form-control" placeholder="Password"
id="password" name="password">
  </div>
</div>
```

For now, we don't include other fields to keep our project simple. Thus, we remove the *image* field.

Next, rename the *submit* button to *Register*.

```
<div class="form-group">
  <button type="submit" class="btn btn-primary">Register</button>
</div>
```

Next in *controllers* folder, create the *newUser.js* controller with the below code:

```
module.exports = (req, res) =>{
    res.render('register') // render register.ejs
}
```

In *index.js*, import the *newUser* controller with:

```
...
const newUserController = require('./controllers/newUser')
```

and apply it to the route:

```
app.get('/auth/register', newUserController)
```

Now, add the 'New User' link in the navigation bar so that one can click to register:

In *views/ layouts/ navbar.ejs*, add:

```
    <div class="collapse navbar-collapse" id="navbarResponsive">
      <ul class="navbar-nav ml-auto">
        <li class="nav-item">
```

```
        <a class="nav-link" href="/">Home</a>
      </li>
      <li class="nav-item">
          <a class="nav-link" href="/posts/new">New Post</a>
      </li>
      <li class="nav-item">
        <a class="nav-link" href="/auth/register">New User</a>
      </li>
    </li>
    </ul>
  </div>
```

The above will then call *newUserController* to render *register.ejs*. If you run your app now and click on 'New User' in the navigation bar, you will be brought to the *register* view (Do note to provide a new image for the background).

User Model

For user registration, we need a user model to represent our *Users* collection just as what we had for *BlogPost*. In *models* folder, create a new file *User.js* and copy/edit contents from *BlogPost.js* to create the *User* schema:

```
const mongoose = require('mongoose')
const Schema = mongoose.Schema;

const UserSchema = new Schema({
  username: String,
  password: String
});

// export model
const User = mongoose.model('User',UserSchema);
module.exports = User
```

Our model is now able to save users. Let's setup the route that is going to be called when a user tries to register an account. Go to *index.js* and register a new route with:

```
...
const storeUserController = require('./controllers/storeUser')
...
```

```
app.post('/users/register', storeUserController)
...
```

Because we have registered the route as */users/register*, in *register.ejs*, specify this same route in the form action of the register user form:

```
<form action="/users/register" method="POST" enctype="multipart/form-data">
```

Handle User Registration

We now create *storeUser.js* for our *storeUserController* to handle user registration.

In *controllers* folder, create a new file *storeUser.js* with the following code:

```
const User = require('../models/User.js')
const path = require('path')

module.exports = (req,res)=>{
    User.create(req.body, (error, user) => {
        res.redirect('/')
      })
}
```

If you run your app now and create a new user with the new user form, there will be a new user document in the database under the *users* collection (fig. 10.1).

```
_id: ObjectId("5cceff9ce46eb16793888814")
username: "user1"
password: "pwd1"
__v: 0
```

Figure 10.1

Notice that our password is currently in plain text which is very insecure. We will need to hash the password before we store it in MongoDB.

Password Encryption

We will use a mongoose model hook to encrypt a password before storing it. A hook is just like a middle ware. We first install a package called *bcrypt* (https://www.npmjs.com/package/bcrypt) to help us hash passwords. Install it using:

```
npm i --save bcrypt
```

Now in */models/User.js*, add the below codes:

```
const mongoose = require('mongoose')
const Schema = mongoose.Schema;
const bcrypt = require('bcrypt')

const UserSchema = new Schema({
  username: String,
  password: String
});

UserSchema.pre('save', function(next){
    const user = this

    bcrypt.hash(user.password, 10, (error, hash) => {
      user.password = hash
      next()
    })
})

const User = mongoose.model('User',UserSchema);
module.exports = User
```

Code Explanation

```
const bcrypt = require('bcrypt')
```

First, import the *bcrypt* package in *User.js*

```
UserSchema.pre('save', function(next) {
  ...
}
```

Next, with *UserSchema.pre('save'...*, we tell Mongoose that before we save any record into the *Users* schema or *Users* collection, execute the function passed into the 2nd argument. This lets us change user data before saving it into the database.

*Note that we have to specify *function(next)* instead of using the lambda short form of a function i.e. next => {...}. I am not too sure why the lambda short form doesn't work.

```
UserSchema.pre('save', function(next) {
    const user = this

    bcrypt.hash(user.password, 10,  (error, hash) => {
      user.password = hash
      next()
    })
})
```

In the function, we first get the user being saved with *const user = this*. mongoose makes the *UserSchema* available via *this*.

We then proceed to call *bcrypt.hash* whose first argument takes in the password to be hashed. The second argument specifies the number of rounds of hashing to take place. For example, we have specified 10 which means that the password will be encrypted 10 times. You can of course specify 100 or more times. The more rounds of hashing there are, the more secure it is but the slower the process too.

The third argument is the function that is called when the hash completes. *user.password = hash* replaces the original password with its encrypted version. We then call *next()* so that mongoose can continue creating the user data.

Now try creating a new user in your app and in the database, you should see an encrypted password (fig. 10.1):

```
_id: ObjectId("5ccfcbec4dc45d748bc5d85b")
username: "user23"
password: "$2b$10$wH4GjdrA1S3w8kNylZIbxux641R6NzqhDkG90wv32317eXVbA.qkK"
__v: 0
```

Figure 10.1

Mongoose Validation

We have used mongoose to help us encrypt our password. Another important feature of a form is to validate user entered data before storing it in the database. When creating new documents, mongoose can help us validate the data before saving it to the database. We do this in the schema. For example, *UserSchema* is currently:

```
...
const UserSchema = new Schema({
  username: String,
  password: String
});
...
```

Suppose we want to ensure that the username is required and unique in the database, we do:

```
const UserSchema = new Schema({
  username: {
    type: String,
    required: true,
    unique: true
  },
  password: {
    type: String,
    required: true
  }
});
```

That is, we pass in a *config* object for each field and specify validation rules in it. In the config object, we have the *required* field that specifies that the field is required. We apply this to both the username and password field. For username, we set *unique* to true, Mongoose will thus check that username should be unique for that record before saving it to the database.

If we run our app and register a user without these fields or if username is not unique, we will see that there is no newly created user in the database. But a problem we have now is that when a user is not created due to failure in field validation, no notification is provided to the user. That is, one might assume that the user has been added when in reality it has not. Later on, we will see how to notify validation errors to the user on the page. But for now, we log the errors to the console.

To log the errors, simply go to *storeUser.js* and add *console.log(error)* as shown:

```
const User = require('../models/User.js')
const path = require('path')

module.exports = (req,res)=>{
    User.create(req.body, (error, user) => {
        console.log(error)
        res.redirect('/')
    })
}
```

Now if we try to add a username which already exists, we get the error logged:

```
...
'E11000 duplicate key error collection: my_database.users index:
username_1 dup key: { : "..." }'
...
```

Having errors logged in the console obviously is not ideal as a person using our app can't (and doesn't want to) refer to the logs! We will later display the error notification in the page itself. But for now, when there is an error, we will redirect back to the user register form with the following code:

```
...
module.exports = (req,res)=>{
    User.create(req.body, (error, user) => {
        if(error){
            return res.redirect('/auth/register')
        }
        res.redirect('/')
    })
}
```

User Login Process

Having created our user register page, we next create a login page. In *views* folder, create a new file *login.ejs*. *login.ejs* will be similar to *register.ejs* so copy the code from *register.ejs* into *login.ejs*. The following steps should be familiar to you.

In *login.js*, change the page heading and button label to 'Login':

```
<div class="page-heading">
  <h1>Login</h1>
</div>
...
<div class="form-group">
  <button type="submit" class="btn btn-primary">Login</button>
</div>
```

Next in form action, change from `<form action="/users/register"`... to:

```
<form action="/users/login"...
```

and in *controllers* folder, create a new file *login.js* with the following code:

```
module.exports = (req, res) =>{
    res.render('login')
}
```

index.js

Next in *index.js*, import the login controller with:

```
const loginController = require('./controllers/login')
```

. . .

and register the route with :

```
...
app.get('/auth/login', loginController);
...
```

Finally, we add *login* to the navbar by going to *view/layouts/navbar.ejs*:

```html
<ul class="navbar-nav ml-auto">
  <li class="nav-item">
    <a class="nav-link" href="/">Home</a>
  </li>
  <li class="nav-item">
      <a class="nav-link" href="/posts/new">New Post</a>
  </li>
  <li class="nav-item">
    <a class="nav-link" href="/auth/login">Login</a>
  </li>
  <li class="nav-item">
    <a class="nav-link" href="/auth/register">New User</a>
  </li>
</ul>
```

Note that the *Login* item has been placed before the *New User* item as this adhers to a user interface design principle where the more frequently used item should be placed first, and one is likely to use the login item more than register a new user.

Login Process

In this section, we implement the login process to compare password and re-direct to the home page if the login is successful. First in *controllers* folder, create a new file *loginUser.js* with the following code:

```js
const bcrypt = require('bcrypt')
const User = require('../models/User')

module.exports = (req, res) =>{
    const { username, password } = req.body;

    User.findOne({username:username}, (error,user) => {
      if (user){
        bcrypt.compare(password, user.password, (error, same) =>{
          if(same){ // if passwords match
            // store user session, will talk about it later
            res.redirect('/')
          }
```

```
        else{
          res.redirect('/auth/login')
        }
      })
    }
    else{
      res.redirect('/auth/login')
    }
  })
}
```

Code Explanation

```
const bcrypt = require('bcrypt')
const User = require('../models/User')

module.exports = (req, res) =>{
    const { username, password } = req.body;
```

We import the *bcrypt* package and *User* model. Next, we extract the username and password from the user login form with *req.body*.

```
    User.findOne({username:username}, (error,user) => {
      if (user){
        ...
      }
      else{
        res.redirect('/auth/login')
      }
    })
```

We then use *User.findOne* to try to find just one user with the inputted username. If such a user exists, we proceed on to compare passwords. If the user doesn't exist, we direct back to the login page.

```
      if (user){
        bcrypt.compare(password, user.password, (error, same) =>{
          if(same){
            res.redirect('/')
          }
          else{
```

```
                res.redirect('/auth/login')
            }
        })
    }
```

To compare passwords, we use *bcrypt.compare* to compare the entered password with the hashed user password retrieved from our database. Note that we use *bcrypt.compare* instead of a equality check e.g. ===. This is to keep us safe from a hacker trick called a timing attack.

If the passwords match, we redirect to the home page where you can see the list of blog posts. If the passwords don't match, we redirect back to the login page.

loginUserController

To apply our *loginUserController*, in *index.js*, import it using

```
const loginUserController = require('./controllers/loginUser')
```

and create a route

```
app.post('/users/login',loginUserController)
```

The route should be the same as that in *form action* back in *login.ejs*.

Now try running your app and log in. You should be re-directed back to the login page if login is unsuccessful and directed to the home page if the login is successful.

Summary

We created a user registration form to add users to our *Users* collection in the database. The *bcrypt* package was used to hash user passwords before storing them. We use Mongoose validation to validate user entered data. We then implement the login process to compare passwords and allow the login when authentication is successful.

Refer to https://github.com/greglim81/express_chap10 for the source code of this chapter.

CHAPTER 11: USER AUTHENTICATION WITH EXPRESS SESSIONS

Sessions are how we keep the user logged into our web app by keeping their information in the browser. Each time a user makes a request, information of that user is sent back to the server. The server thus knows which user is making that request and if they are logged in or out. The information kept on the user's browser is called cookies.

To implement Express sessions, we install a middleware package called *express-session* (https://github.com/expressjs/session):

```
npm install --save express-session
```

Next, import this middleware in *index.js* with:

```
...
const expressSession = require('express-session');
...
```

And add the below:

```
...
app.use(expressSession({
  secret: 'keyboard cat'
}))
...
```

In the above code, we register the *expressSession* middleware in our app and pass in a configuration object with a value to *secret* property. *secret* string is used by the *express-session* package to sign and encrypt the session ID cookie being shared with the browser. You can of course provide your own *secret* string.

Now go to Chrome, refresh your app, and in *Developer Tools*, go to the 'application' tab, and under *Cookies*, localhost domain, you will see that we have a *connect.sid* which contains a hashed value (fig. 11.1). This value is the hashed session ID exchanged with the server and the user's browser telling us which user is currently logged in.

107

Figure 11.1

If you comment the above *express-session* code, clear cookies and refresh the app, you won't see this cookie.

Implementing User Sessions

To implement user session, in *loginUser.js*, add the following line:

```
const bcrypt = require('bcrypt')
const User = require('../models/User')

module.exports = (req, res) =>{
    const { username, password } = req.body;

    User.findOne({username:username}, (error,user) => {
      if (user){
        bcrypt.compare(password, user.password, (error, same) =>{
          if(same){
            req.session.userId = user._id
            res.redirect('/')
          }
          else{
            res.redirect('/auth/login')
          }
        })
      }
      else{
        res.redirect('/auth/login')
      }
```

108

```
    })
}
```

We assign the user _id to the session. The *session* package saves this data on the user's browser so that each time the user makes a request, this cookie will be sent back to the server with the authenticated id. This is how we know if a user is logged in.

To see exactly what is in a session object, go to *home.js* in *controllers* folder and add the following line

```
const BlogPost = require('../models/BlogPost.js')

module.exports = async (req, res) =>{
    const blogposts = await BlogPost.find({})
    console.log(req.session)
    res.render('index',{
        blogposts
    });
}
```

When you log in to your app and get to the home page, you will see that the session has cookie data with *userId* information e.g.:

```
Session {
  cookie:
   { path: '/',
     _expires: null,
     originalMaxAge: null,
     httpOnly: true },
  userId: '5cd0db98f874cd8270bb31fc' }
```

userId will be shared within the server and browser. Thus, in each request, the server will know if the user is logged in or not.

To implement checking for a session id before allowing a user to create a blog post, in newPost.js, implement the following:

```
module.exports = (req, res) =>{
  if(req.session.userId){
    return res.render("create");
```

```
    }
    res.redirect('/auth/login')
}
```

We check if the session contains a user id. If it does, then show the create post page. If it doesn't, redirect back to the login page.

Protecting Pages with Authentication Middleware

Now that we have authentication, we will protect pages that we don't want assessed by users not logged in. For example, we only want logged in users to access the 'post new' page.

First, we create a custom middleware in */middleware/authMiddleware.js* with the following code:

```
const User = require('../models/User')

module.exports = (req, res, next) => {
    User.findById(req.session.userId, (error, user ) =>{
      if(error || !user )
        return res.redirect('/')

      next()
    })
}
```

In it, we fetch the user from the database with *User.findById(req.session.userId...*
We then check if the user is retrieved successfully or if the user doesn't exist, which we direct back to the home page. If the user is a valid user, we permit the request and carry on with *next()*.

Now to apply this middleware, in *index.js*, import *authMiddleware* with:

```
const authMiddleware = require('./middleware/authMiddleware);
```

and in the existing route definition for */posts/new*, pass the middleware in:

```
app.get('/posts/new',authMiddleware, newPostController)
```

You can see the above as a pipeline going from left to right where we call *authMiddleware* before calling *newPostController.*

We apply the same for store post:

```
app.post('/posts/store', authMiddleware, storePostController)
```

With this, an unauthenticated user can't access the new post form and submit a blog post. To test out your app, first delete the existing session from your browser. And when you try to create a new post before logging in, you should be redirected to the home page.

Prevent Login/Register if Logged In

Currently if a user is logged in, they can still visit the login or new user page which shouldn't be the case. Similar to what we have for allowing only logged in users to create posts, we will create a middleware to check if the user is authenticated, and if so, prevent him from accessing the login/new user page.

In *middleware* folder, create the file *redirectIfAuthenticatedMiddleware.js* with the following code:

```
module.exports = (req, res, next) =>{
  if(req.session.userId){
    return res.redirect('/') // if user logged in, redirect to home page
  }
  next()
}
```

The above code should be familiar to you. Next in *index.js*, import *redirectIfAuthenticatedMiddleware* with:

```
const redirectIfAuthenticatedMiddleware =
require('./middleware/redirectIfAuthenticatedMiddleware')
```

Next, apply it to the following four routes:

```
app.get('/auth/register', redirectIfAuthenticatedMiddleware, newUserController)
app.post('/users/register', redirectIfAuthenticatedMiddleware,
storeUserController)
app.get('/auth/login', redirectIfAuthenticatedMiddleware, loginController)
app.post('/users/login',redirectIfAuthenticatedMiddleware, loginUserController)
```

Now when you are logged in, you will be redirected to the home page when you click on Login or New User.

Conditionally Display New Post, Login and New User links

Continuing from the above section, other than redirecting to the home page whenever a logged in user clicks on Login or 'new user', we should hide the new user and login links if a user is already logged in.

To do so, in *index.js* add:

```
...
global.loggedIn = null;

app.use("*", (req, res, next) => {
    loggedIn = req.session.userId;
    next()
});
...
```

Code Explanation

```
global.loggedIn = null;
```

We first declare a global variable *loggedIn* that will be accessible from all our EJS files. Because the navigation bar exist in all our EJS files, they will each have to access *loggedIn* to alter the navigation bar.

With *app.use("*", (req, res, next) => ...*, we specify with the wildcard *, that on all requests, this middleware should be executed. In it, we assign *loggedIn* to *req.session.userId*.

Now, go to *views/layout/navbar.ejs* and use an *if* statement around the new post, login and register route.

navbar.ejs

```
...
        <div class="collapse navbar-collapse" id="navbarResponsive">
          <ul class="navbar-nav ml-auto">
            <li class="nav-item">
              <a class="nav-link" href="/">Home</a>
            </li>
```

```
<% if(loggedIn) { %>
<li class="nav-item">
    <a class="nav-link" href="/posts/new">New Post</a>
</li>
<% } %>
<% if(!loggedIn) { %>
<li class="nav-item">
  <a class="nav-link" href="/auth/login">Login</a>
</li>
<li class="nav-item">
  <a class="nav-link" href="/auth/register">New User</a>
</li>
<% } %>
</ul>
</div>
```

If *loggedIn* is null, we display the *login/new user* links and hide the 'new post' link. If *loggedIn* has a value, i.e. the session id, we hide Login and 'new user' and display the 'new post' link. And because all pages includes *navbar.ejs*, it will apply across all pages.

User Logout

Currently, a logged in user can't log out. Let's create a route for a user to logout. In *navbar*, add the following:

```
...
<% if(loggedIn) { %>
<li class="nav-item">
    <a class="nav-link" href="/posts/new">New Post</a>
</li>
<li class="nav-item">
  <a class="nav-link" href="/auth/logout">Log out</a>
</li>
<% } %>
...
```

The above code displays the Log out link only if a user is logged in. We also specify the route for the logout link as */auth/logout*.

Next, go to *index.js* and create the route and its controller. Create the log out controller in a new file */controllers/logout.js* with the code:

```
module.exports = (req, res) =>{
  req.session.destroy(() =>{
    res.redirect('/')
  })
}
```

With *req.session.destroy()*, we destroy all session data including the session user id, we then redirect to the home page.

We next apply the logout controller to *index.js* with:

...
```
const logoutController = require('./controllers/logout')
```
...

and apply the middleware to the route:

```
app.get('/auth/logout', logoutController)
```

If you run your app now, you will be able to log out with all session data removed.

Creating a 404 page for Non-Existing Route

We currently have no 404 page for a non-existing route. That is, say we type *//localhost:4000/sdfsfs*, We get a "Cannot GET / sdfsfs" error. Typically, websites serve a '404 not found' page whenever a user goes onto an undefined route. In the following, we will create a '404 not found' page for undefined routes.

In *views* folder, create the file *notfound.ejs*. Copy content from any existing EJS page as a starting template and change its *h1* header to "404 page not found". In my case, I have copied from *login.ejs*.

Next in *index.js*, after registration of all routes at the end of the file, add:

...
```
app.get('/posts/new',authMiddleware, newPostController)
app.get('/',homeController)
app.get('/post/:id',getPostController)
```

```
app.post('/posts/store', authMiddleware, storePostController)
app.get('/auth/register', redirectIfAuthenticatedMiddleware,
newUserController)
app.post('/users/register', redirectIfAuthenticatedMiddleware,
storeUserController)
app.get('/auth/login', redirectIfAuthenticatedMiddleware,
loginController)
app.post('/users/login',redirectIfAuthenticatedMiddleware,
loginUserController)
app.get('/auth/logout', logoutController)
app.use((req, res) => res.render('notfound'));
```

With this middleware like route, Express will go through all the routes and if it can't find one that matches, it will render the *not found* page.

Now try entering an undefined route like *//localhost:4000/sdfsfs* and you should see the *notfound* page rendered (fig. 11.2).

Figure 11.2

Summary

We used sessions with the *express-session* middleware to keep users logged in to our app by keeping their information stored in the browser and then sending that information to the server each time a user makes a request. We protect pages reserved for logged in users with an authentication middleware and conditionally display 'New Post', 'Login' and 'New User' links based on if a user is logged in or out. We also created a 404 page for non-existing routes.

Refer to https://github.com/greglim81/express_chap11 for the source code of this chapter.

CHAPTER 12: SHOWING VALIDATION ERRORS

Currently when we have errors in form submission, we do not display them to the user but just redirect them to another page. This is inappropriate as it doesn't inform the user that they have entered invalid data. They might think that what they have entered has gone through successfully when in fact, the process has failed. A better solution would be to straightaway display validation errors to the user so that they can re-submit. In this chapter, we will see how to show validation errors in forms.

Currently in *storeUser.js*, we have the following code:

```
const User = require('../models/User.js')
const path = require('path')

module.exports = (req,res)=>{
    User.create(req.body, (error, user) => {
        if(error){
            return res.redirect('/auth/register')
        }
        res.redirect('/')
    })
}
```

The *error* object actually provides us with validation error notifications that we can work with to display the errors. Let's console log the *error* object to explore what we have and work with that.

For example, if I submit an empty new user form, I get the following errors:

```
errors:
 { username:
   { ValidatorError: Path `username` is required…
     message: 'Path `username` is required.',
     name: 'ValidatorError',
     …
   },
 password:
   { ValidatorError: Path `password` is required…
     message: 'Path `password` is required.',
```

```
    name: 'ValidatorError',

    ...
  }
 },
 _message: 'User validation failed',
 name: 'ValidationError' }
```

That is, *error* would contain a list of individual validation error objects with keys 'username' and 'password' which are the respective fields that have validation errors. If *username* is filled in and valid, we will have just the error key for password.

We now format the errors so that we can present them to the user. Because *Object.keys(error.errors)* gives us all the keys in the *errors* object, we can do the following to get the individual error messages:

```
const User = require('../models/User.js')
const path = require('path')

module.exports = (req,res)=>{
    User.create(req.body, (error, user) => {
        if(error){
            Object.keys(error.errors).map(key =>
error.errors[key].message)
            return res.redirect('/auth/register')
        }
        res.redirect('/')
    })
}
```

We map through the *error.errors* array keys and for each of them, access the key's error *message* property. If you log them to the console, you get something like:

```
[ 'Path `username` is required.',
  'Path `password` is required.' ]
```

Displaying Validation Errors in Template

How do we make the messages available to the view when we redirect using *return res.redirect('/auth/register')*? We do so by assigning the error messages to a variable and saving it to our session with the below codes in **bold**:

```
...
module.exports = (req,res)=>{
    User.create(req.body, (error, user) => {
        if(error){
            const validationErrors = Object.keys(error.errors).map(key =>
error.errors[key].message)
            req.session.validationErrors = validationErrors
            return res.redirect('/auth/register')
        }
        res.redirect('/')
    })
}
```

And in *controllers/newUser.js*, we retrieve the errors from the session with *req.session.validationErrors* and pass it into *register.ejs*:

```
module.exports = (req, res) =>{
    res.render('register',{
        errors: req.session.validationErrors
    })
}
```

Next in *register.ejs*, we display the error messages at the top of our form with the below code placed above *form action*:

```
  <!-- Main Content -->
  <div class="container">
    <div class="row">
      <div class="col-lg-8 col-md-10 mx-auto">
        <% if(errors != null && errors.length > 0){ %>
          <ul class="list-group"></ul>
            <% for (var i = 0; i < errors.length; i++) { %>
              <li class="list-group-item list-group-item-danger"><%=
errors[i] %></li>
            <% } %>
          </ul>
        <% } %>
        <form action="/users/register" …>
          ...
```

First, we check that the *errors* array passed in from *newUser.js* is not null and has at least one error item. If *errors* is null or its empty, it means that there is no error and we can continue with the form submission. If there is at least one item in the *errors* array, we loop through it and for each error, we display them with the ***class="list-group-item list-group-item-danger"*** to make the error appear danger red (fig. 12.1).

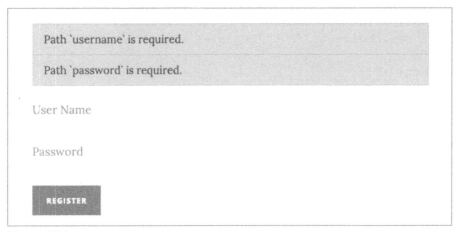

Figure 12.1

*For more information on styling list items, refer to
https://getbootstrap.com/docs/4.0/components/list-group/

Now when you run your app, try submitting the 'new user' form and if there are any validation errors, it will appear to the user in danger red.

Duplicate Entry Error

We meet with one critical error however, if we enter a non-unique user, e.g. *user1* which already exists in the database, our app crashes. This is because we get a Mongoose validation error when you attempt to violate a unique constraint, rather than a *E11000* error from MongoDB.

The *mongoose-unique-validator* package helps us makes such error handling easier. First install the package:

```
npm install --save mongoose-unique-validator
```

and then apply it to */models/User.js* with the codes in **bold**:

```
const mongoose = require('mongoose')
```

```
const Schema = mongoose.Schema;
var uniqueValidator = require('mongoose-unique-validator');

const bcrypt = require('bcrypt')

const UserSchema = new Schema({
  username: {
    type: String,
    required: true,
    unique: true
  },
  password: {
    type: String,
    required: true
  }
});

UserSchema.plugin(uniqueValidator);
...
```

Now when we try to save a user, the unique validator will check for duplicate database entries and report them just like any other validation error (fig. 12.2).

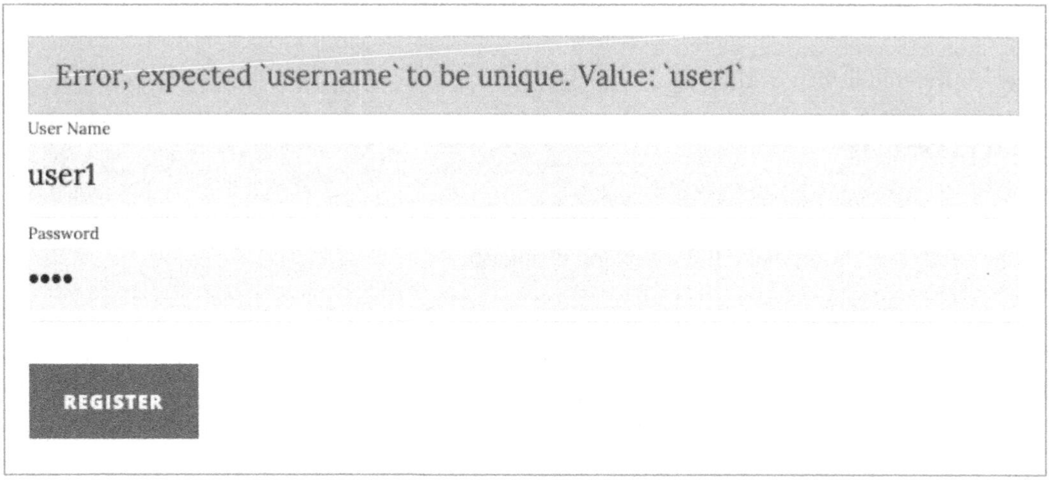

Figure 12.2

Flushing Error Messages from Session

Because we are saving the error messages in the session however, and because a session is permanent, it means that in the next request life cycle the session will still be there. That is, the error notifications are not flushed away when the user re-visits the form after a successful submission.

Thus, we need the *errors* data to expire after the current request lifecycle and this is what we refer to as *flushing*, where we don't want the data to be available after the next request. We will do this with a package called *connect-flash* (https://www.npmjs.com/package/connect-flash). *connect-flash* provides a special area of the session used for storing messages. Messages can be written to this area and cleared after being displayed to the user.

First, install *connect-flash* using:

```
npm install connect-flash
```

In *index.js*, import the package:
```
...
const flash = require('connect-flash');
...
```

Then register the middleware with:
```
...
app.use(flash());
...
```

Next in *controllers/storeUser.js*, make the following changes:
```
...
module.exports = (req,res)=>{
    User.create(req.body, (error, user) => {
        if(error){
            const validationErrors = Object.keys(error.errors).map(key =>
                error.errors[key].message)
            req.flash('validationErrors',validationErrors)
            //req.session.validationErrors = validationErrors
            return res.redirect('/auth/register')
        }
        res.redirect('/')
```

```
        })
}
```

With the *flash* middleware, all requests will have a *req.flash()* function that can be used for flash messages. In *flash()*, we specify that validation errors will be stored in the 'validationErrors' key.

To retrieve the errors and present them in the view, make the changes in *newUser.js*:

```
res.render('register',{
    //errors: req.session.registrationErrors
    errors: req.flash('validationErrors')
})
```

That is, we retrieve errors from the **'validationErrors'** key and make them available to this view to be displayed after which the flash is cleared.

Now when you run your app and there are form validation errors, the page errors are only there after the form is first submitted. The errors are no longer there when the page is refreshed. Thus, we have achieved where a user should only see errors for that specific request made. This is flushing, where the validation errors are only available for the next request life cycle and in the following cycle, is deleted.

Customising Error Messages

Currently, the error being shown to the user is not very useful as its too technical for them to understand (fig. 12.3).

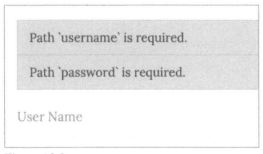

Figure 12.3

We should be providing clearer error messages like 'Please provide *username*' for them to rectify the error. To provide customized messages, go to *models/User.js* schema and make the following change:

models/User.js

```
const UserSchema = new Schema({
  username: {
    type: String,
    required: [true,'Please provide username'],
    unique: true
  },
  password: {
    type: String,
    required: [true,'Please provide password']
  }
});
```

That is, *required* accepts an array where we pass in the customized message in the 2nd argument.

Now we get the customized validation message (fig. 12.4):

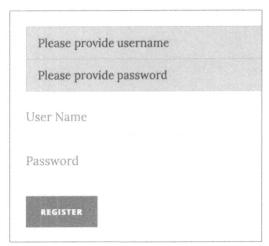

Figure 12.4

Persist Request Data on Form

Currently when the user fills in data into the form, tries to submit it and there is an error, all the data keyed in is removed and the user has to re-type the data in. A better user experience would be that the data keyed in should stay and not be removed even if there have been validation errors.

To keep the data keyed in, we also flash *req.body* which contains the data keyed into the form. In *controllers/storeUser.js*, add the following line:

```
const User = require('../models/User.js')

module.exports = (req,res)=>{
    User.create(req.body, (error, user) => {
        if(error){
            const validationErrors = Object.keys(error.errors).map(key =>
            error.errors[key].message)
            req.flash('validationErrors',validationErrors)
            req.flash('data',req.body)
            return res.redirect('/auth/register')
        }
        res.redirect('/')
    })
}
```

We store *req.body* in the 'data' key of flash. Next in *controllers/newUser.js*, add the codes in **bold**:

```
module.exports = (req, res) =>{
    var username = ""
    var password = ""
    const data = req.flash('data')[0];

    if(typeof data != "undefined"){
        username = data.username
        password = data.password
    }

    res.render('register',{
        errors: req.flash('validationErrors'),
        username: username,
        password: password
    })
}
```

If we try logging *req.flash('data')* to the console, we realize that *req.flash('data')* returns us an array with the data in the first element. Thus we access it using *req.flash('data')[0]*. We then check if *req.flash('data')* is undefined which will be the case whenever we first visit the new user form. If it's not undefined, only then we assign the *username* and *password* fields. Note that the *username* and *password* fields are initialized with a blank string. This is to avoid the form from throwing an error saying that the value is null or undefined.

Now that we have sent *username* and *password* values to *register.ejs*, in it, fill in the data values into *value* property of the *<input>* tags:

```
...
<input type="text" class="form-control" placeholder="User Name"
name="username" value="<%= username %>">
...
<input type="password" class="form-control" placeholder="Password"
name="password" value="<%= password %>">
...
```

When you run the app now and the user fills in data in the form, tries to submit it and there is an validation error, the data keyed in will be preserved and the user doesn't have to re-type the data in.

Refer to https://github.com/greglim81/express_chap12 for the source code of this chapter.

Exercise

Now that you have implemented form validation, display of validation errors and persisting form data,
- implement the same for the create blog post form
- also implement the notification of error when a login is unsuccessful in the login form (due to incorrect username or password).

CHAPTER 13: RELATING POSTS COLLECTION WITH USERS COLLECTION

Currently, we have not linked users with their posts together. We will now link the *Users* and *Posts* collection together. In *models/BlogPost.js*, change *username* to *userid* with an object:

```
...
const BlogPostSchema = new Schema({
  title: String,
  body: String,
  //username: String,
  userid: {
    type: mongoose.Schema.Types.ObjectId,
    ref: 'User',
    required: true
  },
  datePosted:{
    type: Date,
    default: new Date()
  },
  image: String
});
...
```

userid contains an object with properties *type*, *ref* and *required*. In *type*, we specify *mongoose.Schema.Types.ObjectId* which means that the value is supposed to be a valid Mongo object id. As mentioned previously, Mongo has a specific id for each document and they have to be in a valid format. In *ref*, we specify *User* to refer to the *User* collection which the document is contained.

Next in *storePost.js*, add the following line:

```
...
module.exports = (req,res)=>{
    let image = req.files.image;
    image.mv(path.resolve(__dirname,'..','public/img',image.name),async
(error)=>{
        await BlogPost.create({
```

```
        ...req.body,
        image: '/img/' + image.name,
        userid: req.session.userId
    })
    res.redirect('/')
  })
}
```

That is, we assign *userid* as **req.session.userId**. Remember that *req.session.userId* is populated with the logged in user id in *loginUser.js* when a user logs in.

Now when you run your app, log in and submit a blogpost, the post document will have the *userid* field populated.

However, the *username* now doesn't show up in the "Posted by ..." in the blog post excerpt (fig. 13.1). This is because we have replaced *username* with *userid*.

Figure 13.1

In the next section, we will see how to appropriately populate the post with its user data.

Display Post with User Data

Our *posts* collection is now linked to the users collection. Each post stores a reference to the user (*userid*) who created that post. With *userid*, we will then populate the post with the user data.

In *controllers/home.js*, call the *populate('userid')* method of *schema.find({})* as shown:

```
const BlogPost = require('../models/BlogPost.js')
```

```
module.exports = async (req, res) =>{
    const blogposts = await BlogPost.find({}).populate('userid');

    console.log(req.session)
    res.render('index',{
        blogposts
    });
}
```

*BlogPost.find({}).**populate('userid')*** automatically references the specified document with the *userid* in the collection.

So now, in *views/index.ejs*, under 'Posted by' make the following change:

```
...
<p class="post-meta">Posted by
            <a href="#"><%= blogposts[i].userid.username %></a>
...
```

When you run your app, you might get an error because some of your old blog posts do not yet have the *userid* field because the ***userid: req.session.userId*** code wasn't yet in place. In this case, you might need to drop the entire *blogposts* collection in MongoDB Compass Community by clicking on the dustbin icon. A pop up will appear asking you to confirm the deletion by typing in the collection name (fig. 13.2).

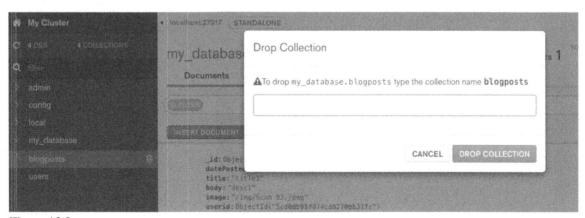

Figure 13.2

When you do so, the collection will be deleted. Now, submit a new blog post and when you go to the home page, the username will be populated.

We have to do a similar change in the individual blog post page. Go to *controllers/getPost.js*

```
const BlogPost = require('../models/BlogPost.js')

module.exports = async (req,res)=>{
    const blogpost = await BlogPost.findById(req.params.id).populate('userid');
    console.log(blogpost)
    res.render('post',{
        blogpost
    });
}
```

Again, we call the *populate* method of *findById*.

In *views/post.ejs*, change to *blogpost.**userid.username*** to have the username appear.

```
...
<span class="meta">Posted by
                <a href="#"><%= blogpost.userid.username %></a>
...
```

Summary

In this chapter, we linked our *users* and *posts* collection together with the *schema.find.populate* method which references the document in the specified collection.

Refer to https://github.com/greglim81/express_chap13 for the source code of this chapter.

CHAPTER 14: ADDING A WYSIWYG EDITOR

Currently, our create blogpost form is just a plain text form. We will now add a 'What you see is what you get' - WYSIWIG editor for a user to format his blog post in exactly the style he wants it. To do so, we will make use of a nice HTML editor (https://summernote.org/) that we can attach to our blog post form (fig. 14.1).

Figure 14.1

To embed the editor in our create post form, go through the instructions at https://summernote.org/getting-started/#for-bootstrap-4. In it, there's an example of how to embed the editor into your page. We first need to copy the following lines into the header of our page:

```
<script src="https://code.jquery.com/jquery-3.2.1.slim.min.js"></script>
<script
src="https://cdnjs.cloudflare.com/ajax/libs/popper.js/1.11.0/umd/popper.min.js"><
/script>
<script src="https://maxcdn.bootstrapcdn.com/bootstrap/4.0.0-
beta/js/bootstrap.min.js"></script>
```

```
<link href="https://cdnjs.cloudflare.com/ajax/libs/summernote/0.8.12/summernote-
bs4.css" rel="stylesheet">
<script src="https://cdnjs.cloudflare.com/ajax/libs/summernote/0.8.12/summernote-
bs4.js"></script>
```

Recall that our header is specified in */views/layout/header.ejs* which is included by all other pages. Thus, we should add the above in *header.ejs*. But if we do so, the scripts will be available to all pages which would be unnecessary and add to our loading time. We should make the scripts accessible only to the page to create a post i.e. *create.ejs*.

To do so, in *controllers/newPost.js*, we have an additional boolean *createPost* which is set to true in *newPost.js*.

```
module.exports = (req, res) =>{
  if(req.session.userId){
    return res.render("create",{
      createPost: true
    });
  }
  res.redirect('/auth/login')
}
```

That is, *createPost* will only exist and equals *true* when a user visits the route */posts/new*. In *views/layouts/header.ejs*, we add an *if* to check if *createPost* is defined and is true, then we include the related summernote scripts:

```
<!-- Custom styles for this template -->
<link href="/css/clean-blog.min.css" rel="stylesheet">
<% if(locals.createPost && createPost) { %>
  <script src="https://code.jquery.com/jquery-3.2.1.slim.min.js"></script>
  … other scripts for summer note
<% } %>
</head>
```

Note that the *locals* object contain properties that are local variables within the application. Thus, to test if *createPost* is defined, we check for *locals.createPost*.

Lastly in *views/create.ejs*, in the place where we want the editor to appear, we declare a custom id (I have chosen *body*) and add the <script> as shown below:

```
<div class="control-group">
  <div class="form-group floating-label-form-group controls">
```

```
<label>Description</label>
<textarea id="body" name="body" class="form-control"></textarea>
<script>
  $('#body').summernote({
    placeholder: 'Hello bootstrap 4',
    tabsize: 2,
    height: 200
  });
</script>
</div>
</div>
```

Now, when you go to the create post page, the summernote editor should appear (fig. 14.2).

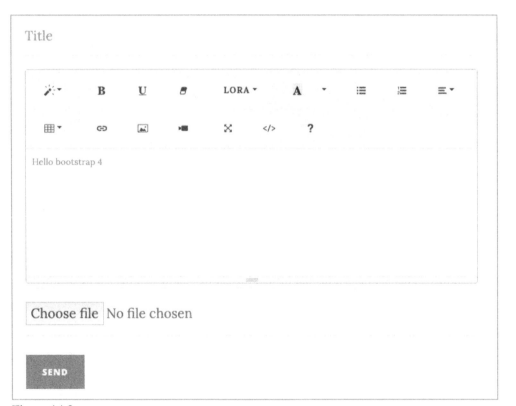

Figure 14.2

And if you visit other pages and see the page source code, the summernote scripts will not be there. Only in the create post page will the summernote scripts be in the page source.

Now you can create posts with various formats (fig. 14.3).

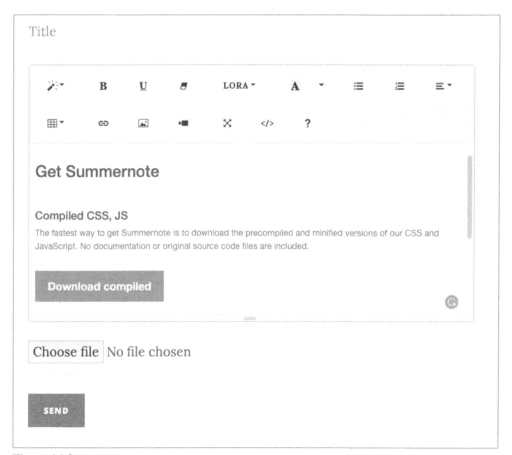

Figure 14.3

After the post is submitted however, the post still doesn't appear formatted well. This is because we have not told the templating engine to format the content as HTML instead of text.

To tell EJS to render the content as HTML instead of text, in *views/post.ejs*, simply specify <%- ...%> as shown below:

```
<!-- Post Content -->
<article>
  <div class="container">
    <div class="row">
```

```
    <div class="col-lg-8 col-md-10 mx-auto">
        <%- blogpost.body %>
    </div>
  </div>
</article>
```

Summary

We added a WYSIWYG editor for our create blog post form to format the blog post in the manner a user wants it.

Refer to https://github.com/greglim81/express_chap14 for the source code of this chapter.

.

CHAPTER 15: USING MONGODB ATLAS

Currently, we go to *localhost:4000* to access our website because our local computer is acting as the server to serve up the information to our website. We are also running a MongoDB server in our local computer. Though this is great for development and testing of our apps, no one else can currently access our website over the Internet.

In this chapter, we explore using MongoDB's own cloud service *MongoDB Atlas* to host our database on the cloud and in the next chapter, we will see how to host our Node.js server on *Heroku* so that we can deliver our website over the Internet.

Setting Up MongoDB Atlas

First, sign up for a MongoDB Atlas account (https://www.mongodb.com/download-center). Under 'Deploy a free cluster', create a new account and click 'Get started free' (fig. 15.1).

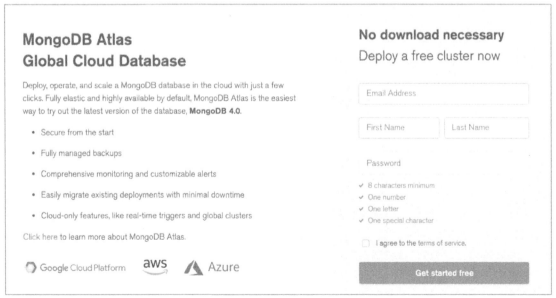

Figure 15.1

You will be brought to a 'Build a New Cluster' page. Under 'Global Cluster Configuration', choose 'AWS' as cloud provider (because they provide a free account without having to enter credit card details). Under 'North America', select 'North Virginia' where we can get a free tier for our MongoDB (fig. 15.2).

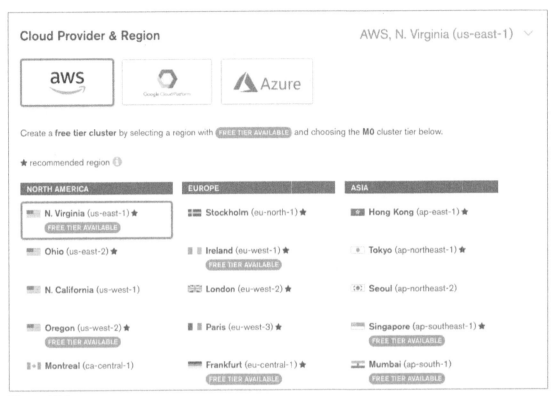

Figure 15.2

Next under 'Cluster Tier', choose the 'M0' free tier (fig. 15.3).

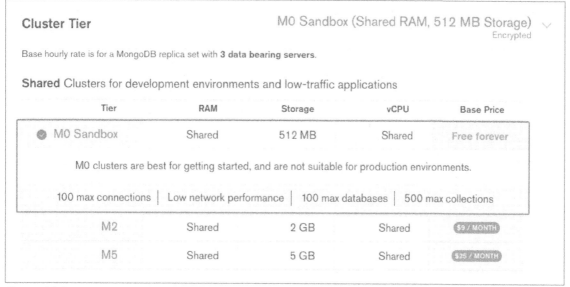

Figure 15.3

The good thing about Amazon AWS is that we can experiment without having to worry about making unintentional mistakes and getting a huge bill from Amazon. When your website gets more popular with more users, you can then scale up at a later stage. Keep the other default options and select 'Create Cluster.' It will prompt you saying that it takes 7-10 minutes to set up everything on AWS (fig. 15.4).

Figure 15.4

Next, on the left panel, under 'Security', click on 'Database Access' where you do not yet have a user. Create a database user by clicking on 'Add New User' and provide him with 'Read and write to any database privileges' (fig. 15.5).

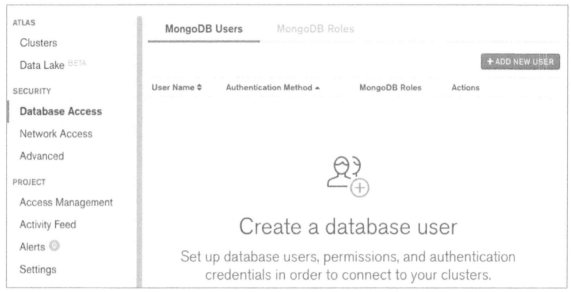

Figure 15.5

Next, under 'Security', 'Network Access', 'IP Whitelist', select 'Add IP Address' and choose 'allow access from anywhere' (fig. 15.6).

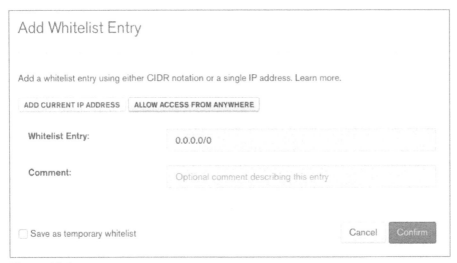

Figure 15.6

Next, we will connect with MongoDB Compass. Back in the dashboard, under the cluster we just created, click on 'Connect' (fig. 15.7).

Figure 15.7

Select 'Connect with MongoDB Compass'.

In the next form that pops up, because we already have Compass, go ahead to specify your version and copy the connection string to a text-editor and replace <password> with the newly added database user password. Next, copy the enter connection string again (fig. 15.8).

Figure 15.8

Next in Compass, in the top bar, select 'Connect', 'Connect to...' and paste the connection string in. In fact, Compass might prompt you that it has detected a connection string in the clipboard and auto populate it for you (fig. 15.9). Click 'Connect' and it will then connect to the MongoDB Atlas Cloud Cluster.

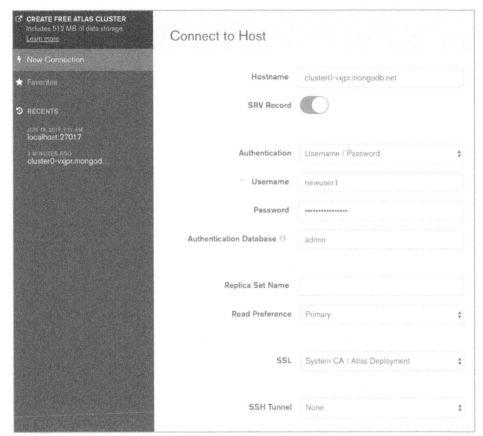

Figure 15.9

Once connected, in MongoDB Compass, click on 'Create Database' and create a database with the collection 'BlogPosts' (fig. 15.10).

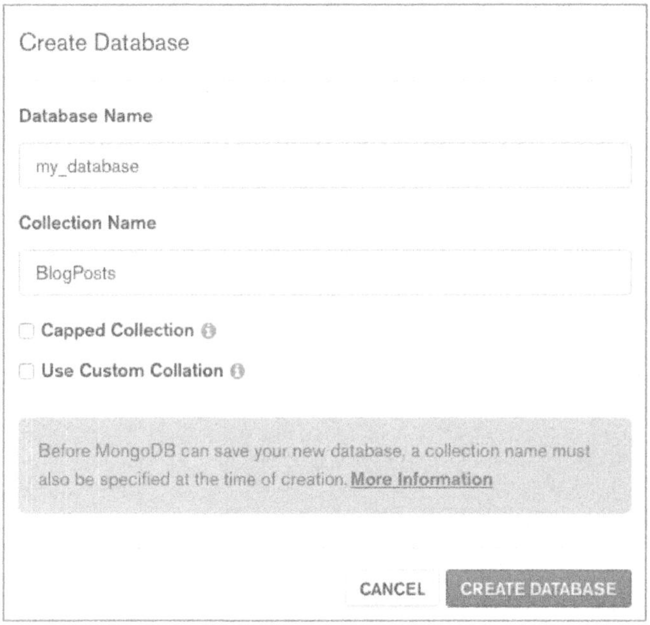

Figure 15.10

Now that we have connected to the MongoDB Atlas Cloud cluster from Compass, we will next need to connect it from our app.

When starting our app on a local machine, we ran the MongoDB server locally. Now that we are using the cloud cluster, we can terminate the local MongoDB server instance *mongod* on our machine.

And in *index.js*, we have to change the connection string from

```
mongoose.connect('mongodb://localhost/my_database', {useNewUrlParser:
true});
```

to (fill in your own database username, password and database name):

```
mongoose.connect('mongodb+srv://newuser1:<your_password>@cluster0-
vxjpr.mongodb.net/my_database', {useNewUrlParser: true});
```

Now run your app and you will realize that all previously added users and blog posts are gone because we have connected to a new database hosted on the cloud. So, go ahead and add a new user, login and then create some blog posts. Then go back to Compass to see that the user and blog post records have been added to the cloud database!

In the next chapter, we will deploy our app on Heroku to make our app accessible from anywhere on the Internet.

CHAPTER 16: DEPLOYING WEB APPS ON HEROKU

Heroku allow us to deploy our Node.js app on to the Internet. We will be deploying our code to Heroku's servers who will host and run our Node.js, Express application which connects to our cloud MongoDB Atlas database. The deployment process is relatively straightforward and you can simply follow along the instructions in the documentation to deploy Node.js apps on Heroku (https://devcenter.heroku.com/ - fig. 6.1). But we will still walk you through the deployment process in this chapter.

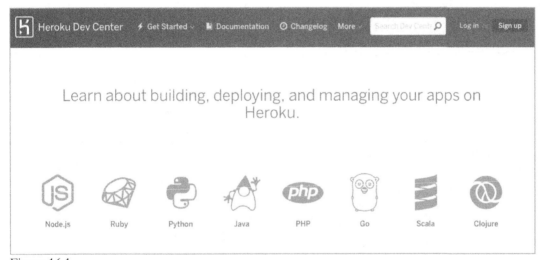

Figure 16.1

First, you will need a Heroku account. So, go ahead and sign up if you don't have an account.

Next, we need to install the Heroku Command Line Interface for creating and managing our Express apps on Heroku (fig. 16.2).

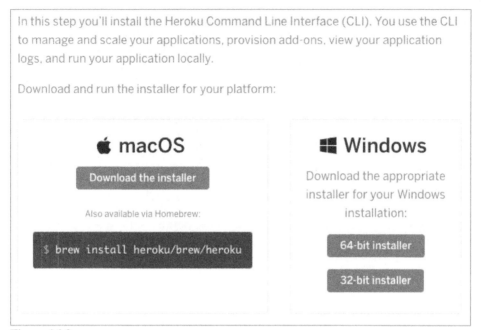

In this step you'll install the Heroku Command Line Interface (CLI). You use the CLI to manage and scale your applications, provision add-ons, view your application logs, and run your application locally.

Download and run the installer for your platform:

Figure 16.2

When the installation completes, we can start using the *heroku* command from our Terminal. Type *heroku login* and a web browser will be opened to the Heroku login page (fig. 16.3).

```
$ heroku login
heroku: Press any key to open up the browser to login or q to exit
 >    Warning: If browser does not open, visit
 >    https://cli-auth.heroku.com/auth/browser/***
heroku: Waiting for login...
Logging in... done
Logged in as me@example.com
```

Figure 16.3

If the browser is already logged into Heroku, click 'Log In'.

Making our App 'Heroku Ready'

Before we start deploying to Heroku, we have to make our app 'Heroku ready'. We do so in the following sections by:
- adding a Procfile
- adding our Node.js version to *package.json*
- listening on the correct port and
- specify the *.gitignore* file

148

Add a Procfile

In our app directory, create a file named *Procfile* (capital *P*, without a file extension). This file will be run when Heroku starts our app. In our simple app, this file will only be one line. Copy the below line into *Procfile*:

```
web: node index.js
```

web refers to the process type (the only process type that can receive HTTP traffic from the web). The command after *web* i.e. *node app.js* is run on the Heroku server just as what we have done to run our app on the local machine.

package.json

Next, add the version of Node.js that your app requires in *package.json*. That is, find out the version of Node you are running using *node --version*, and add it to your *package.json* like in the below code in **bold**:

```
...
  "license": "MIT",
  "engines":{
    "node": "10.15.3"
  },
  "author": "Start Bootstrap",
  "contributors": [
    "David Miller (http://davidmiller.io/)"
  ],
...
```

This tells Heroku that our app requires Node 10.15.3 for example.

Listening on the Correct Port

Because Heroku sets up an environment variable *process.env.PORT* for the port, we have to specify this in *index.js* where we do *app.listen*.

That is, currently we are doing:

```
app.listen(4000, ()=>{
    console.log('App listening on port 4000 ...')
})
```

Replace this with:

```
let port = process.env.PORT;
if (port == null || port == "") {
  port = 4000;
}

app.listen(port, ()=>{
    console.log('App listening...')
})
```

This ensures that our app on Heroku is listening on the port specified by `process.env.PORT`.

.gitignore

Next, if we have not already done so, create a file *.gitignore* in our app directory. This file tells Git to ignore whatever is specified in it from being pushed onto the server. And because we don't need to push *node_modules*, add `node_modules` to *.gitignore*

With these steps, our app is now 'Heroku ready' and we can go ahead to deploy our app.

Deployment

For deployment, if you haven't already, you need to have the *git* version control system installed. Install *git* by following the instructions in https://git-scm.com/book/en/v2/Getting-Started-Installing-Git and then setting up *git* for the first time (https://git-scm.com/book/en/v2/Getting-Started-First-Time-Git-Setup).

When *git* is installed and setup, set up a *git* project in the app's root directory with:

```
git init
```

Next, use:

```
git add .
```

to add all of our project files. Then to commit the changes to your Git project, run:

```
git commit -m "Initial commit"
```

You will see in the logs something like:

```
Created initial commit 5df2d09: My first commit
 44 files changed, 8393 insertions(+), 0 deletions(-)
 create mode 100644 README
 create mode 100644 Procfile
```

```
create mode 100644 app/controllers/source_file
...
```

Next, run:

```
heroku create
```

This creates a new empty application on Heroku with an associated empty Git repository. A new URL for your Heroku app will also be setup (fig. 16.4).

```
$ heroku create
Creating app... done, ● thawing-inlet-61413
https://thawing-inlet-61413.herokuapp.com/ | https://git.heroku.com/
```

Figure 16.4

You can change the URL or associate a domain name you own with the Heroku address but it is beyond the scope of this book.

Now, we push our code to the remote Git repository that we have just created with:

```
git push heroku master
```

This will push the code to the Heroku servers and setup our app's dependencies on them. Going forward when there are code changes in our app, run *git push heroku master* again to re-deploy.

And if you go to the URL that was generated for you, you will see your app running on the Internet (fig. 16.5)!

Figure 16.5

Final Words

We have gone through quite a lot of content to equip you with the skills to create a Node.js, Express and MongoDB app.

Hopefully, you have enjoyed this book and would like to learn more from me. I would love to get your feedback, learning what you liked and didn't for us to improve.

Please feel free to email me at support@i-ducate.com to get updated versions of this book.

If you didn't like the book, or if you feel that I should have covered certain additional topics, please email us to let us know. This book can only get better thanks to readers like you.

If you like the book, I would appreciate if you could leave us a review too. Thank you and all the best for your learning journey in Node.js, Express and MongoDB development!

About the Author

Greg Lim is a technologist and author of several programming books. Greg has many years in teaching programming in tertiary institutions and he places special emphasis on learning by doing.

Contact Greg at support@i-ducate.com or http://www.greglim.co/

ONLINE COURSE VERSION

www.greglim.co

This book is all you need to learn Node.js, Express and MongoDB development. But if you are a more visual learner and learn better from absorbing this book's content through an online course, you can get access to the book's online course version **free** by contacting support@i-ducate.com and providing a proof of purchase.

The course content is the same as this book. So, if learning through books is your preferred way of learning, skip this. But if you prefer to learn from videos (and you want to hear my voice), you can visit the following link:

www.greglim.co

Made in United States
North Haven, CT
23 December 2021

13565181R00085